# REVOLUTIONS

By Chip Zielke

# REVOLUTIONS

A comprehensive guide to "keeping your game on track"
with Bowling equipment.

Second Printing

ISBN 0-9646144-0-5



Layout and Printing by:
Jostens Printing and Publishing
David O'Brien - Representative
(410) 515-0202

Illustrations by:
Hillustrations, Inc.
Michael Hill
(410) 893-7620

This book was produced using Aldus PageMaker 5.0 and Adobe Illustrator 5.5.



Inquires may be directed to:

Revolutions International
21035 Homeland Road
Matteson, Illinois 60443

# WHAT ROLE DOES EQUIPMENT PLAY IN THE SPORT OF BOWLING?

I believe every bowler will agree that this is a valid question. Given today's bowling ball market, there are many decisions which need to be made concerning a new balls reaction and economics. Will the most expensive ball always provide the best reaction? Depends.

What is important, is the understanding that bowling equipment only comprises 1/5th of the total equation of a complete bowling game. This is often times forgotten, as bowlers are always being told that a new bowling ball will solve their various liabilities on the bowling lanes.

In studying the game of bowling, you must realize that there are 5 main areas that an improving, high average or world class player must become skilled in if they are to succeed in the bowling game. These are as follows;

## PHYSICAL GAME

- Having the correct Timing and Armswing for your game, and the ability to make adjustments to each based on conditions.
- Having 2 or 3 effective releases.
- Maintaining the ability to "Repeat Shots."

## LANE PLAY

- Understanding how to play all of the "Angles" from the "Outside Shot" to the "Track Shot" to "Deep Inside" and the "Fallback."
- Understanding how to Make Spares on all conditions.
- Targeting to a "Breaking Point" as well as the dots or arrows, and visualizing the "Shape" of each shot.

## BOWLING BALLS

- Determining the best "Grip" for you.
- Matching the cover of the ball to your needs on specific conditions.
- Balancing the ball dynamically based on the lane conditions and your game.
- Developing the right combination of bowling balls for a variety of conditions based on your game.

## MENTAL GAME

- How to prepare for a competition.
- Staying "Focused" and "In the Game".
- Having the ability to motivate and relax when needed.
- Having a "Mental Plan".

## PHYSICAL CONDITIONING

- Maintaining good physical fitness for strength and endurance
- Providing good "fuel" for your body before during and after the competition

# WHO WILL BENEFIT FROM THIS BOOK?

If you are a beginner, intermediate, or advanced bowler, this book will help. You will gain knowledge for determining the best equipment for your particular game, and how to put it to good use. If you are searching for answers with your bowling equipment, you have most likely competed in our sport for a period of time. Hence, if bowling equipment is your nemesis, this book will help to fortify that area of your game.

Too often, bowlers become confused not only with all of the new equipment on the market, but also with their current set of bowling balls. Many players carry two or four bowling balls, but do not understand how each should react. This book will provide you with a game plan for your bowling equipment. Thus, to know how each of your current bowling balls should react, and how to make a new ball fit into your equipment package.

Also, one of the biggest misconceptions in our sport is that a new $150.00 bowling ball will give us those needed extra pins in our average, or help us to make the "cut" in our next tournament. True, if the bowler has a sound fundamental game, is accurate to a reasonable degree, and can make spares, than the ball has a good chance to help. However, if these initial criteria are not met, there is no doubt that the $150.00 would be better spent in practice games or lessons with a certified instructor.

If you find that you need additional help with the other areas mentioned, there are a few options available. The advent of USA Bowling, and their certification courses, have produced many qualified instructors available to help in improving your physical game. I encourage you to seek out these coaches and schools for further improvement, if and when needed. I do not know of any sport where the athletes do not depend on a coach, or group of coaches to develop their skills. Bowling is no different.

But for now, I suggest that you forge on. Lets explore the "equipment" portion of our great sport in the following pages. Plus, while you are gaining knowledge through this book, seek out good instruction, work hard, and the dividends will pay off!

# ACKNOWLEDGMENTS

I would like to thank and acknowledge the people responsible for helping me to learn the sport of bowling, and who have ultimately contributed to this book.

The single most influential person responsible for much of my equipment knowledge is Ray Edwards. Ray, is without a doubt, the foremost expert in our sport on dynamic balance and bowling ball development. Ray has had to endure hundreds of questions from this author over the course of the last 12 years, and has and still does patiently answer them to the best of his ability. For all of his efforts I am very grateful.

There are four people who have truly taught me how to study our great sport and have also had a tremendous influence on my career. They are: Jeri Edwards, Fred Borden, Don Johnson, and Sam Baca. Along with Ray Edwards, it is my firm belief that collectively, this group of people represents the greatest wealth of bowling knowledge in the world.

I would also like to thank Julie Emerson for her faith and confidence when including me on the Professional Bowling Camps staff in the early 1980's. It is through this program that I have evolved as an instructor and learned a greater appreciation for our sport.

Kathy and I have some very special friends around the world who have encouraged this project and helped it to become a reality. They include; Michael Fiaux, Eric Chambettaz and Michael Dewarrat from Switzerland; Sheik Abdulrehman Bin Mubarak Bin Hamed Alkhalifa, Tariq Khalifa and Hasan Rasool Hasan from Bahrain; and C.H. and Carol Loy from Singapore. To all of you and the many other friends we have outside of the U.S., Thank You.

In any endeavor, a persons family is a great source of strength and encouragement. Our families are no exception. It is through their support over the years that we have had the freedom to strive for our goals, with the knowledge that they would be there for encouragement when it is needed. Thank You all.

CHIP ZIELKE

# DEDICATION

I would like to dedicate this book to all of the athletes in our great sport who are hungry for knowledge, devoted to learning, and that strive for perfection. I would also like to dedicate this to those people in the bowling industry especially committed to raising the level of awareness of bowling, and who work for the betterment of our sport. I wish you all of the best and encourage you to remain focused and dedicated.

One person who epitomizes these aforementioned characteristics is someone very dear to me. This person has sacrificed many years in learning, improving and contributing to our sport and has been a great influence on my career. Few people would endure the frequent travel, relocations and all of my theorizing, which have helped me to grow and learn as a coach, instructor and person. For this and much more I would like to say "thank you" and also dedicate this book to my wife, Kathy.

# *Table of Contents*

## Revolutions

# Achieving a Better Grip on your Bowling Equipment

## Chapter 1

How many sports, when you stop to think about it, involve putting your hand into the object you are to use in the sport? The only one that comes to my mind is bowling. Lets analyze....

Football has laces on the ball to help maintain a firm grip, and allow the ball to be thrown easier. Baseballs have a seam which allows the players a better grip on the ball. Basketballs have dimples for the same purpose. Soccer balls are kicked. Golf and Tennis are activities which the ball is struck with another object, and are not gripped by the hand.

Bowling is really the only sport which involves putting your hand into the object which is to be used in the activity.

Since people of all ages, physical builds, athletic skill levels, and vocations compete in our sport, it would make sense that almost everyone will need to have their bowling ball custom fit to their hand.

*For example...*

A 6'3" 250lb male construction worker would probably not have the same grip drilled into a bowling ball as a 5'2" 115lb female school teacher. (I don't think they would use the same weight ball either!)

As we are different and unique people, it makes sense that many factors will come into play when a Pro Shop Professional begins the fitting process. Some of these factors include:

Flexibility or Stiffness in the joints of your hand
Length of the fingers and thumb
Webbing at the base of the thumb
Dry or moist skin
Grip strength
Physical injuries or ailments (such as arthritis)

As a bowler, you are not required to understand all the intricacies of fitting. However, you should seek out a Pro Shop which pays close attention to these factors.

# ANALYZING THE GRIP

In this chapter, we will discuss the three main components of the grip:

Hole Sizes
Span
Pitches

No matter how many ways you try to study the grip, it always comes down to these three areas. Whatever your skill level, the grip is one of the most important elements in the physical bowling game.

# HOLE SIZES

When a person first learns to bowl, the usual procedure is to find a ball from the ball storage racks that matches closely to the size of their fingers and thumb. Unfortunately, the typical "house ball" has holes drilled on the large size to accommodate many bowlers. As we mentioned earlier, people come in all shapes and sizes, and these balls need to fit as many people as possible!

If you don't remember this yourself, you can witness this scenario any Saturday night at your local center. Recreational players are always scurrying around, trying to find a ball they can hold onto without dropping, and something they will be able to release at the moment of truth.

As funny as it sounds, the sad reality is that the same thing can happen to you when you purchase a new ball. Discount sporting goods stores are notorious for drilling 3 holes into the ball, all the same size, and expecting it to fit your hand perfectly!

The good news is that most Pro Shops, which specifically drill bowling balls, will have a fitting ball with all available hole sizes. This allows you and the ball driller to determine which holes are going to fit your fingers and thumb the best.

## THE USE OF BOWLING TAPE

You may have experienced a time when you have had a bowling ball custom fit and drilled, in which the hole sizes seemed to change. What you need to be aware of is that you and your environment may change, which can alter the feel of the ball in your hand. Consider the following factors:

Personal weight loss or gain
Seasons changing (winter to summer)
Inside temperature of the bowling center
Intense competition

These factors are all things that can seem to make the holes "change" in size. The most widely used method of making minor grip adjustments is by using tape. Many of the leading manufacturers sell tape specifically designed for use in your finger and thumb holes. This allows you to attain a comfortable "feel" every time you bowl.

A good general rule with the use of tape is to put the more "coarse" or abrasive tape in the front of the hole, and the smooth tape at the back. Also, make sure you put the tape on the front and back of your fingers and thumb, not side to side. Putting tape on the sides can inhibit your release by making your hand stay in the ball too long. By placing the tape in the front and back of the holes, you can insure yourself of a clean and consistent release shot after shot.

Also, don't be afraid to change the tape during your league or tournament competition. Many times you will be on a pair of lanes with air conditioning blowing on you, or in an intense game where you may sweat more. These examples can have a direct effect on your grip and release, and should be taken care of immediately.

Finally, the message is make the grip holes feel comfortable (not too tight or not too loose). Whether you are buying a new ball, or trying to make an existing ball feel good, use tape or have your pro shop plug and redrill the hole to the proper size.

## SPANS

In all of bowling there are three commonly used spans or grips. These are:

Conventional
Fingertip
Semi Fingertip

## SPAN CONSIDERATIONS

The criteria for a properly fit Fingertip or Conventional Grip includes:

Thumb fully inserted to its base
Fingers fully inserted to, but not beyond a joint, depending on the grip
Palm against the ball
Wrist straight

As we will identify with all three types of grips, the first element, thumb fully inserted into the ball is very important. Regardless of any span, the thumb represents the greatest gripping power that we have on the ball. For example, if the thumb is only halfway into the hole, we have considerable less gripping strength. This can cause injuries to the bowling arm, and problems with our timing and armswing in our overall physical game. Therefore, it is very important that this initial criteria is met during the fitting process.

Next, *fingers fully inserted to, but not beyond a joint, depending on the grip is also very important.*

There is a simple test which you can perform on either your fingertip or conventional grip ball to check if the span is of correct length. Simply insert your thumb fully into the thumb hole, and lay your fingers across the holes. (You need to do this while keeping your wrist straight). The test is to see where your finger joint rests in relation to the holes.

Ideally, for a conventional grip, the second finger joint (from the nail) should lay close to the center of the hole. (within 1/8 - 3/16 of an inch either above or below center is usually acceptable, depending on the size of your hand). For a fingertip grip, the first finger joint (from the nail) should rest between 1/8 of an inch past the front edge of the hole (edge of the hole closest to the thumb hole) to the middle of the hole.

If you find the joint does not reach the aforementioned position in relation to the holes, and for example only reaches the front edge (closest to the thumb hole) of the hole, the span is considered long. Just the opposite, if the joint goes past center to the opposite edge of the hole (furthest from the thumb) the span is considered short. Neither of these is beneficial. Lets look at the problems long or short spans can cause.

## LONG SPAN

Contrary to historical beliefs, long spans can be detrimental. Here is just a few problems that can arise from a long span:

Hand Problems:

- Calluses on the inside base of your thumb
- Calluses on the back of your thumb
- Blood blisters under your finger nails
- Nerve damage in your thumb

Physical Game Problems:

> If span is too long, often this means that the fingers or thumb are not fully inserted to their respective holes. This causes excess gripping to hold onto the ball and can ultimately cause a tight or muscled swing, a low back swing, and ultimately poor timing. Also, long spans make you release the ball in a forward motion, without much rotation. This can cause the ball to begin rolling too soon, and can make it roll out.

## SHORT SPAN

Just like the long span, a short span can also cause problems. Here a just a few:

- Calluses on the back of the thumb
- Muscled swing
- Early release of the ball (dropping ball)
- Overturning the ball

 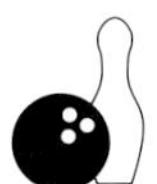

Quite often, short spans make you squeeze to hold onto the ball. This is caused by the uncomfortable feeling that you are going to drop the ball. This is especially true if the holes are a little on the big side. This squeezing is what causes the calluses to appear on the back of the thumb and what can lead to a muscled swing.

Overturning is just the opposite of what happens with a long span. The long span makes you stay behind the ball longer, while the short span promotes early turning of the wrist at the point of release. This is what ultimately creates the early turn and can cause a low track or a spinner effect in the roll pattern.

When using either the Fingertip or Conventional grip, you will want to have as much of the surface of your palm against the ball as possible. This allows for better gripping strength during the approach and release, as well as insuring a proper span.

The one aspect of fitting which is often overlooked is the final criteria, keeping the wrist straight. This needs to be done during the fitting process to insure the correct span is measured. If the wrist is in a "cocked" position during the fitting process (meaning the thumb is at a 6:00 position and the fingers at a 2:00 - 3:00 position for a right-handed player), the span will almost always be long. If you have been fit in this manner, you will notice additional pressure on the ring finger (particularly on the back of the nail) as the wrist is moved to a straight position, with your fingers and thumb in the ball.

Ideally, when gripping the bowling ball, you should have an equal amount of pressure on both fingers when using either the fingertip or conventional grip. This can sometimes be a trial and error process with the bowler and ball driller, but should be achieved during the fitting process. This will help to ensure a comfortable span and overall grip.

## CONVENTIONAL OR FINGERTIP - WHICH IS BEST FOR YOU?

As mentioned earlier, there are three types of grips; Conventional, Semi Finger Tip and Finger Tip. The conventional grip is the most common one for people new to the sport, young people, or senior citizens. This is the easiest grip to use, and gives us the greatest chance to hold on to the ball. The reason being that we have more of our fingers inserted into the ball than the other two types of grips, thus allowing for better control.

As the names of the other two grips imply, they only insert the fingers to the first finger joint (from the nail) or slightly past. The conventional grip involves inserting our fingers into the holes, up to the second joint, and then fully inserting the thumb. This allows for greater gripping power and more control as the ball is swinging through the approach. (figure 1.1)

Bowlers who use the fingertip grip only insert their fingers to the first joint. Initially, this grip feels different because less surface of our fingers are used to grip the ball. However, once the bowler is accustomed to this new grip, they find a greater time difference between when the thumb and fingers release the ball, therefore promoting a greater chance for lift. (figure 1.2)

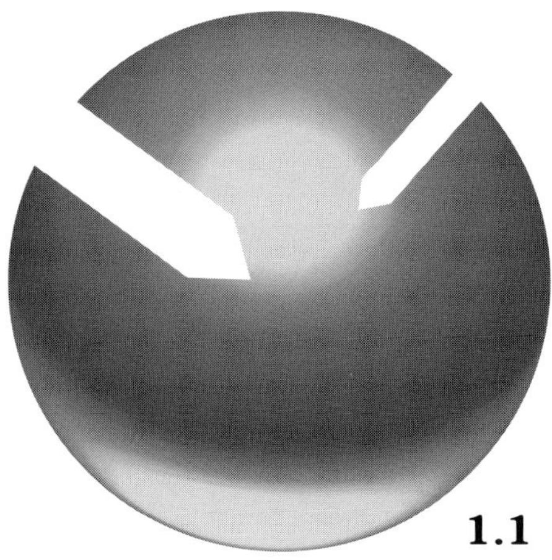

1.1

**Conventional Grip**
The fingers are inserted to the second joint (from the nail), and the thumb is fully inserted to it's base.

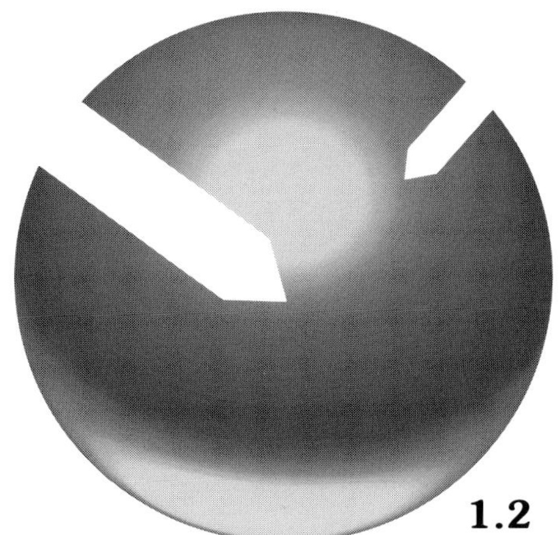

1.2

**Fingertip Grip**
The fingers are inserted to the first joint (from the nail), and the thumb is fully inserted.

To better understand this, lets take a look at the commonly recognized definition of "Lift" in terms of a bowling release.

LIFT - *The time differential from when the thumb releases the ball to when the fingers release the ball.*

To expound on the definition, we actually have two release points. The thumb release and the fingers release. Based on the definition, it is easy to assume that the greater time difference between the thumb and finger releases the more "Lift" or stronger release we will have.

Since we have more of our hand in the ball with the conventional grip, it is understandable that our fingers and thumb must release the ball at almost the same time. Thus equalling less lift. Whereas, with a fingertip grip, we have a longer span, less of our fingers in the ball, and a much greater chance to achieve considerably more lift.

When using the fingertip grip, the bowler can decide how they want to release the ball. They have the option to throw it relatively straight, with a small amount of lift, or they can opt for a larger hook with a different release. Again, as this option is not available with the conventional grip, top players choose the fingertip for the lift, as well as the versatility it gives them. This is why all top amateur and professional players use this type of grip or small variance of it.

## THE SEMI FINGERTIP

The semi fingertip grip is one that is really not recommended. The reason the first two grips are successful is because the fingers are inserted into the holes at a joint. This allows the hand to rest comfortably in the ball and allows the palm to rest against the ball. The semi fingertip involves inserting the fingers to a position between the two finger joints. This is not a natural position. Between those two joints is your finger bone, which unfortunately does not bend. Therefore, with this type of grip, your palm cannot rest fully against the ball as there will be

space created by the fingers not being placed in the holes at a joint. Additionally, it is difficult to find a consistent gripping position and to attain a consistent release. (figure 1.3)

**Semi Fingertip Grip**
The fingers are inserted to a position between the first and second joints (from the nail), and the thumb is fully inserted.

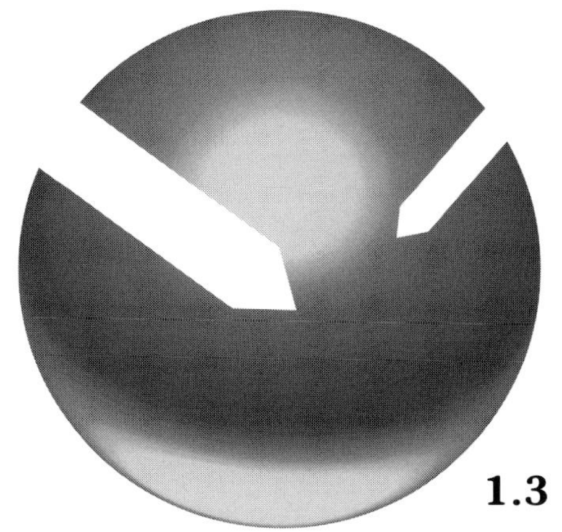
**1.3**

# PITCHES

Pitches, just as spans, have certain considerations which must be satisfied to achieve a properly fit ball. These are as follows;

Flexibility in fingers and thumb
Thumb joint and webbing
Length of span
Grip strength
Type of release

Although hole sizes and the span are very important to the grip of the ball, the pitches are quite possibly the most important element. A ball properly fit to your hand with the correct pitches can be very comfortable to grip, hold through your swing, and release cleanly. A ball fit with improper pitches, however, can be uncomfortable, and can have a drastic effect on your release.

# UNDERSTANDING PITCHES

There are 2 ways we look at pitches, front to back and side to side. Lets start with the pitches front to back, which are commonly referred to as forward and reverse pitch.

One of the easiest ways to understand how these pitches work, is to use the following example.

## FORWARD PITCH

Imagine you are going to grip a softball. To achieve holding the ball, you place your palm against the ball, and bring your fingers and thumb towards your palm (pressing against the ball at the same time). This allows you to have a firm grip on the ball, and you can move your arm without the ball dropping from your hand.

## REVERSE PITCH

To release the ball, you would use the opposite motion. Instead of gripping or bringing your fingers and thumb towards your palm, you would allow these to go away from the palm, thus allowing the ball to drop from your hand.

The forward and reverse pitches work the same way with your bowling ball. The more forward pitch used on your fingers and thumb will help you to grip the ball easier, and delay the release of the ball. Conversely, the more reverse you use on the fingers and thumb will allow you to release the ball faster and earlier.

The figures 1.4 and 1.5 show what forward and reverse pitch look like when drilled into the bowling ball. If the hole is drilled towards the exact geometric center of the ball, the pitch would be considered to be "Zero." (figure 1.6) Therefore, a hole that is drilled more towards the palm, above the zero point, is considered forward pitch. Likewise, if the hole is drilled away from the palm, below the zero point, it would be considered reverse. This holds true for both the finger pitches and the thumb pitch.

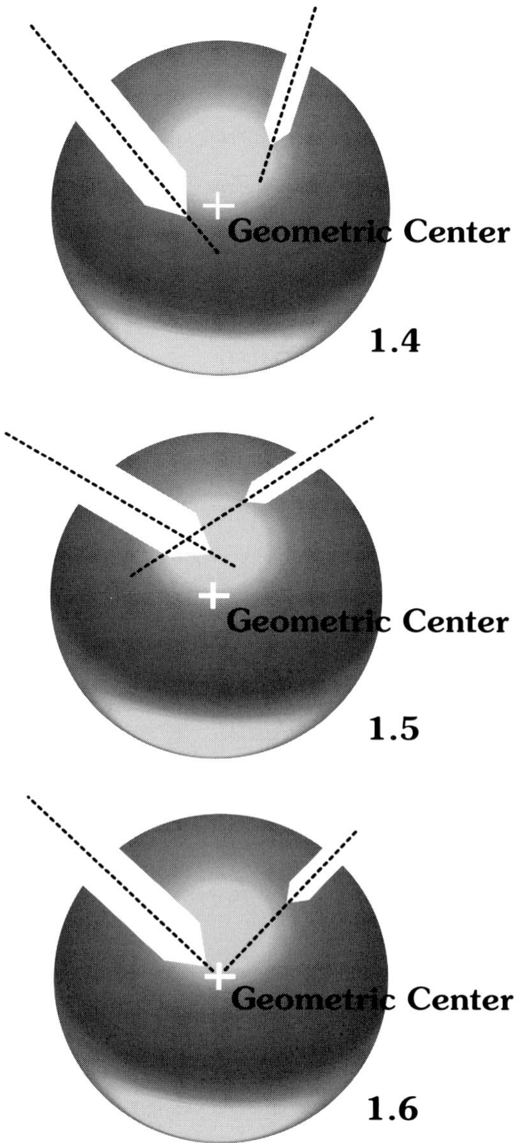


**Reverse Pitch**
Fingers and thumb are drilled away from the geometric center of the ball.

**Forward Pitch**
The fingers and thumb are drilled towards each other, or forward of the geometric center of the ball.

**Zero Pitch**
When the fingers and thumb are drilled towards the geometric center of the ball.

# APPLYING THE "GENERAL RULES" FOR REVERSE PITCH

The one common message throughout this book is that there are no specific rules or ways to accomplishing many things in our bowling game. This is true in ball fitting, physical game, timing, or playing lanes. However, there are many good general rules that we can follow to help us to come close to realizing our goals. The following represent some good general rules for pitches.

Lets look at the general rules for reverse pitch in the thumb;

Flexible thumb and thumb joint
Long thumb
Wet hand
Long span
Hook Ball Player - needing a quick thumb release

The most important factor when dealing with pitches is to identify the flexibility of your fingers and thumb, and grip strength. As we have stated from the beginning of this book, people from all walks of life participate in the game of bowling. Therefore, it would be reasonable to assume that everyone's hand will have different amounts of flexibility.

Some people will have extremely flexible hands, while others (especially those with arthritis) will have very stiff hands. Obviously, these two people would not have the same pitches drilled into their bowling ball.

First, the flexible thumb. As a general rule, these types of bowlers will need more reverse pitch on their thumbs, because their hand naturally wants to move away from their palm in a "reverse" direction. Just the opposite would be a person with a very stiff thumb joint. This person would need less reverse pitch and more of a pitch towards zero or forward. Once again, the reason for this is due to the bowlers hand construction, and lack of flexibility. This factor makes the thumb naturally want to be in a "forward" position.

The next consideration is a long thumb. If you were to compare the thumbs of 10 different people, chances are that you would see a noticeable difference in each persons thumb length. As we have stated, the general rule is, the longer the thumb, the more reverse pitch needed for a clean release. Really, the concept is quite simple. The longer the thumb, the more time the thumb needs to come out of the thumb hole at the time of release. To aid in the longer thumb releasing quicker, increase the amount of reverse pitch, and the thumb will release naturally.

To accompany the concept of a long thumb, a person with a moist or sweaty hand will also need a little more reverse pitch. The moist thumb will "Drag" against the walls of the thumb hole, and delay the release. With increased reverse pitch, the thumb has a much better chance to release at the right time.

The long span is also fairly simple to understand. The more "palm" you have against the surface of the ball, the more your thumb wants to go in a reverse position. Therefore, with a longer span, more reverse is needed to allow the thumb to be placed comfortably, and naturally into the ball. Also, since there is more of the palm against the ball, the palm assists in gripping the ball, much like a basketball player can "Palm" the basketball. Therefore, less of a forward pitch is needed to grip the ball.

More General Rules - This time for forward pitch in the thumb

Flexibility in the thumb and thumb joint
Short thumb
Dry thumb
Short span
Dropping the ball at release

As you can probably surmise, the opposite factors of reverse pitch will be prevalent with forward pitch. However, it is beneficial to understand them as many bowlers need adjustments with both forward and reverse pitch.

As stated earlier, flexible joints usually require more reverse pitch on the thumb. Based on this, less flexible thumbs want to stay in a more forward position. With extremely stiff thumbs, and stiff hands, it is generally recommended to have not only small reverse or forward pitch in the thumb, but also a slightly shorter span to make the grip comfortable.

Short and dry thumbs require a pitch more towards forward, so the bowler can simply have a better grip on the ball. The short thumb has less gripping power, because there is less surface of the thumb against the inside of the thumb hole (as compared to a long thumb). Also, a dry thumb has the tendency to release from the thumb hole quicker, than a moist or sweaty thumb. Therefore, in both cases, less reverse pitch and more towards zero or forward pitch is desirable.

Short spans also require more of a forward pitch in the thumb. Either short fingertip grips or conventional grips mean less of the palm against the surface of the ball (as compared to a previous example of a person with a large hand, fingertip grip, and more of the palm against the ball). In this case, the bowler needs the pitches to assist in gripping the ball. Therefore, a pitch more towards forward would be desirable.

Finally, if a bowler has the problem of dropping the ball at the point of release, or having to squeeze excessively to hold onto the ball, more of a pitch towards forward would be advised. The new pitch will help to grip the ball easier, allowing for a loose armswing and uninhibited release.

## LATERAL THUMB PITCHES

The other pitches previously discussed were the right or left, or more commonly referred to as lateral pitches. Lateral pitches are most concerned with thumb flexibility, and release.

 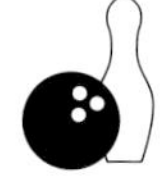

We have discussed thumb flexibility quite a bit up to this point. However, we have only discussed it in a forward or reverse manner. Now we will analyze flexibility from right to left.

One of the easiest ways to test lateral flexibility in the thumb is to have a friend or your Pro Shop operator conduct the following test.

First, have the assistant place their thumb approximately 1/2 inch below the base of your thumb. Then with you relaxing your hand, have the other person put pressure against your thumb to see how far it can comfortably bend towards your palm. This will give you a good general idea of the lateral flexibility in your thumb.

Some bowlers have thumbs that can literally touch their palm when conducting this test. Others cannot bend their thumbs to a straight up (12:00) position.

Lets understand the drilling of lateral pitches. Based on figure 1.8, if the thumb hole is drilled towards the geometric center of the ball, the lateral pitch will be considered "Zero." When the hole is drilled to the right of zero, it is considered "Right" pitch. As you can assume, when the hole is drilled to the left of zero, it is considered "Left" pitch. (figures 1.9 and 1.7)

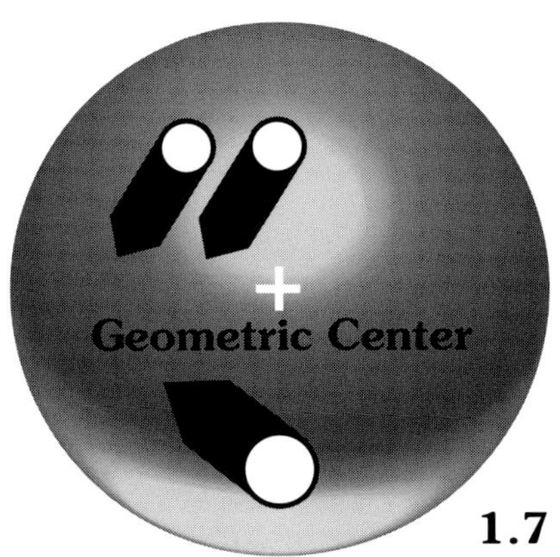


**Left Pitch**
When the finger and/or thumb holes are drilled to the Left of the geometric center of the ball.

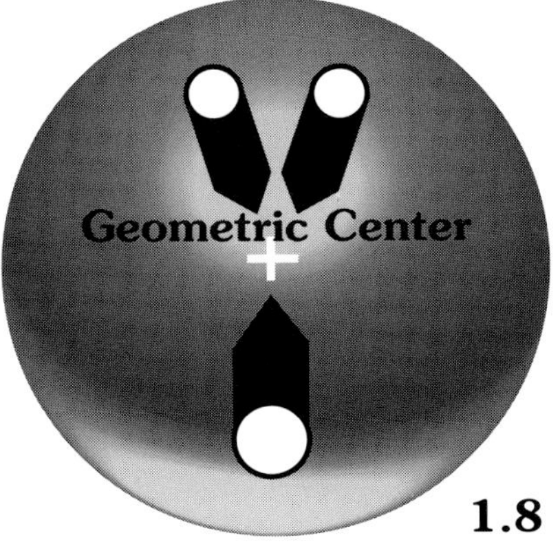


**Zero Pitch**
(Lateral Pitches) When the finger and thumb holes are drilled towards the geometric Center of the ball.

**Right Pitch**
When the finger and/or thumb holes are drilled to the Right of the geometric center of the ball.

Therefore, the less flexible thumb (for right-handed bowlers) will have a pitch more towards zero, or left pitch. Right-handed bowlers with more flexible thumbs will have their thumb pitch more to the right of zero, constituting right pitch. (Left-handed bowlers can reverse the process, more flexible thumb = left pitch while stiffer thumbs require zero or right pitch.) The amount of the pitch is determined by the flexibility or stiffness of the bowlers hand, and can be a trial and error process until a comfortable pitch is achieved.

## FINGER PITCHES

Finger pitches, just like thumb pitches, are mostly focused on flexibility. This is especially important to understand when relating forward and reverse pitch to the fingers. Historically, people assumed that the more forward pitch on the fingers, the more lift you would have. However, this is not necessarily true.

A more realistic view of finger pitches is to match the flexibility in the finger joints with the appropriate pitch. The concept with finger pitches is to achieve the greatest amount of the finger "pad" against the inside of the finger hole. If the finger is stiff and resistant to bending, than trying to put this finger in a hole drilled with forward pitch will not be beneficial. It would be better suited to a hole drilled with more reverse pitch.

Just as in previous examples, if the finger holes are drilled towards the geometric center of the ball, they are considered zero pitch. Holes drilled more towards the palm are considered forward pitch, and holes drilled away from the palm (past zero) are considered reverse.

Therefore, if the finger joint is flexible, forward pitch can be used. However, if the joint is stiff, or only has a small amount of flexibility, than zero or reverse pitch would be the answer.

This simple test for flexibility in your fingers is one you can do without assistance.

First, place the thumb of your opposite bowling hand just below the base of your first finger joint. Then, with your opposite bowling hands index finger, apply pressure against the finger nail. The amount of flexibility will be determined by how much the joint bends. For stiff joints, you will not see much bend. However, with flexible joints you will see quite a lot of bend.

Lateral pitches for the fingers are dependent on 2 factors; finger "shape" and release.

Many people find that one or both of their fingertips point more to the right or left, as opposed to being straight. Therefore, you can adjust the lateral pitches to match the "shape" of your fingertips, and eliminate calluses in the process. (Calluses on the sides of the fingers are usually caused from incorrect lateral pitches).

Concerning the release, some bowlers like the feel of the finger pitches drilled in a way to help them have a greater feel of lift when they release the ball.

For example, a right-handed bowler might pitch the holes laterally to the right for the feeling of extra lift. This would enable the bowler to feel the sides of his fingers lifting against the inside of the ball during release. Left handers would pitch the fingers laterally to the left for the same feel.

Using these lateral pitches for a better feel is really a personal preference.

As always, if you have a question regarding your finger pitches, visit your local pro shop for further assistance.

 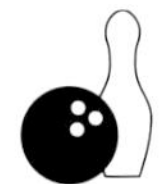

# GRIP ACCESSORIES

The four different types of accessories commonly used with the grip are:

Finger Grips
Thumb Grips
Finger Slugs
Thumb Slugs

Finger Grips are certainly the most common of these accessories. A fair statistic for the number of bowlers using finger grips is between 60 - 80%. This represents a large number of bowlers, and a substantial business for the grip industry. Why are finger grips so popular? Three of the most common reasons are:

Comfort in the finger holes
Additional gripping power
Consistent feel from ball to ball

Many bowlers prefer the feel of the finger grips, opposed to the inside surface of the ball. If this is your preference, it should be fairly easy to find one that will feel comfortable, as grips come in many different textures.

Finger grips also provide an extra amount of gripping power to the ball. Having the softer feel of the grips against the fingers (as opposed to the ball) gives bowlers the feel of a stronger grip. Additionally, many grips come with additional forward pitch in the grip (from 1/8 - 1/4 of an inch extra pitch). This can aid in achieving slightly more lift at the point of release. The key to remember when using these grips with the extra pitch, is to allow for the extra pitch when drilling the finger holes. Lets look at the following example:

When measuring the flexibility in your finger tip, you and your ball driller conclude that you need zero pitch after drilling to attain a proper fit. If the hole is drilled with zero pitch, but then you add a finger grip which has 1/4 of an inch of forward pitch, the net result would be 1/4 of an inch of forward pitch in the finger hole, as opposed to the zero pitch which your finger needs.

This commonly happens when a bowler decides to change grips. For example, the bowler changes from oval grips (with no pitch) to grips with 1/4 of an inch forward pitch. This not only will change the finger pitches, but will alter the "feel" of the overall grip. The key is to check with your ball driller before making any changes which could alter your grip, therefore avoiding any problems the change could create.

Finally, bowlers use these grips at achieve a consistent feel from ball to ball. If a bowler has a 4 ball set, and does not use finger grips, there is a chance the fingers holes will feel different when comparing all 4 balls. The reason is that it is very difficult to work out each ball exactly the same, and very common to have a slightly different feel from ball to ball. Additionally, the texture of the ball will make the inside of the holes feel different (reactive, urethane, polyester). It is for these reasons that bowlers will use finger grips to achieve a more similar feel from ball to ball.

### THUMB GRIPS

Thumb grips are used for basically the same reasons as finger grips. Two main reasons are:

Achieving consistent feel
Reducing bevel work

Achieving consistent feel is much the same as was mentioned with finger grips. Today's bowling balls have different textures on the inside, and can affect grip and release for some bowlers. Thus, for the bowlers who prefer a more similar feel when changing balls, the thumb grips are the answer.

Thumb grips usually come in 2 different configurations; round and ovaled. The type of grip used depends largely on the shape of the bowlers thumb. For bowlers with more of a round thumb, the round grip will work very well. Likewise, bowlers that have a more flat thumb (flat front to back and wider from side to side) will find the oval grips more comfortable. This is where reducing bevel work becomes a factor. Instead of having to custom shape the thumb hole to fit the thumb (which usually never feels the same from ball to ball), a bowler can use the oval grip to reduce the amount of bevel work, and attain a more consistent feel.

The bottom line with grips is to use what feels comfortable. You are the only one who knows what feels best to you. Meaning, if you find that grips help and make the grip more comfortable, then by all means they should be used. However, if you decide that the ball feels better without grips then there is no reason to use them. It's all up to you. There is no right or wrong, only what works best for you!

### FINGER AND THUMB SLUGS

Finger and thumb slugs are generally used for altering the pitches or span of a previously drilled ball. These allow the bowler to make changes immediately, and saves the time of the plugging process.

Also, with the advent of today's reactive resin bowling balls, many bowlers prefer the feel of a thumb slug or thumb grip as opposed to the conventional thumb hole. Some of today's reactive resin balls have more of a "tacky" feeling on the inside of the ball. The grips or slugs allow the bowler to have a smoother feel in the finger or thumb holes, and as previously mentioned, a consistent feel between bowling balls.

## HOW THE GRIP CAN AFFECT YOUR RELEASE

All of the previous information has been given to help identify your base grip. To summarize, the following criteria must be met to achieve your base grip:

Fingers inserted to their appropriate joint
Thumb fully inserted to its base
The span drawn out to its proper length
The grip holes drilled to match the flexibility of the fingers and thumb
As much of the palm against the surface of the ball as possible

Once this base grip has been established, there is a certain amount of flexibility you can introduce to your grip to alter the release and ball roll.

How lateral pitches affect the release
How to create more revolutions on your ball
How to change your ball track

As previously mentioned, lateral pitches need to be established for you base grip. Once established, these can be altered to affect the rotation of your bowling ball. Generally, the parameters from your base grip will range from 1/8 - 1/4 of an inch, depending on the flexibility of your hand. The following examples will help to explain this concept.

## HOW TO INCREASE ROTATION AT THE POINT OF RELEASE

Lets assume you are a right-handed bowler, and your base grip calls for zero lateral pitch in your thumb hole. However, you find that with this pitch, your ball roll is too forward (in an end over end motion) and provides little hook and carry power. One possible solution would be to increase the amount of right pitch by 1/8 or 3/16 of an inch (depending on your hands flexibility) in the thumb hole to allow your hand to "turn" easier at the point of release (you may also need to adjust the reverse pitch of your thumb when making this change). Thus increasing the rotation of your bowling ball and allowing for more hook and hopefully better carrying power.

## HOW TO DECREASE ROTATION AT THE POINT OF RELEASE

In this example, lets assume you are a left-handed bowler whose base grip calls for 1/4 of an inch left pitch in the thumb hole. However, with this pitch, you find that your ball spins too much and does not roll early enough (sometimes this causes the ball track to be low). One possible solution to decrease the rotation and increase the amount of forward roll would be to decrease the amount of left pitch by 1/8 - 1/4 of an inch (again depending on the flexibility of your hand). This would make the thumb pitch closer to zero, and allow your hand to stay behind the ball longer before turning, thus promoting a more forward roll. (You may also need to adjust the amount of reverse pitch on your thumb when making this change).

## KEYS TO INCREASING YOUR REVOLUTIONS

Almost everyone in our sport would like to increase the amount of revolutions they generate on their bowling ball. The important thing to remember, however, is that the bowling ball cannot completely change a poor release. The bowler must be in a strong biomechanical position and have the bowling arm and hand in the appropriate position for a strong release. This factors should be addressed before making adjustments to your grip for more revolutions.

Assuming you have a strong biomechanical position at the point of release, there are a few changes which can be made in your grip to increase the amount of revolutions you can generate on your bowling ball. The major changes come with the amount of forward or reverse pitch in your fingers and thumb.

One way to assist you in increasing your revolutions is to increase the amount of reverse pitch in the thumb and fingers, from your base pitches. Once again, we have the 1/8 - 1/4 of an inch allowance for change based on the hands flexibility. Increasing the amount of reverse pitch will allow the ball to be released faster from the hand, and should increase the amount of revolutions as the ball rolls down the lane (you may have to adjust the amount of lateral pitch in your thumb when making this change). Once again, this will only occur if you are in the correct physical position with your timing, armswing, and hand position.

## CHANGING YOUR BALL TRACK

The final change we will address is the change to your ball track. First, lets define the ball track.

BALL TRACK - *THE PORTION OF THE BALL WHICH COMES IN CONTACT WITH THE LANE AS IT ADVANCES TO THE PINS.*

Usually, the easiest way to identify the ball track is to notice where the oil ring is located on the ball. This is the portion of the ball which has come in contact with the lane, and is easiest to recognize. Most bowlers will usually fall into one of the following 3 categories in terms of their ball track;

Semi or 3/4 Roller
Spinner
Full Roller

The most common of the three is the first, the semi or 3/4 roller. This ball track has become recognized as the most effective track given the lane surfaces and oiling patters upon which bowlers presently compete. The most "sought after" roll is one where the track is approximately 1" from both the fingers and thumb (figure 1.10).

**Semi Roller or 3/4 Roller**
**Ball Track**

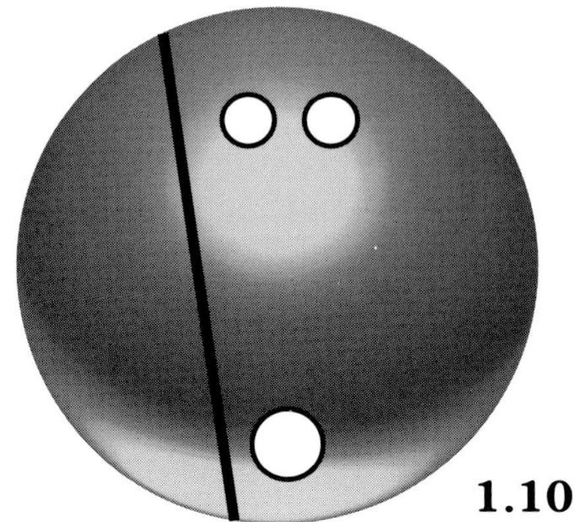

**1.10**

Unfortunately, many people find themselves trapped into trying to attain the "perfect" ball track. What they fail to realize is that there are many World Champion bowlers who have ball tracks that are far less than perfect. As the old adage says, its not how, its how many.

A spinner type ball track is considered to be 3 inches or further from the grip (figure 1.11). To achieve a strong ball roll, it is advantageous to have more of the balls surface come in contact with the lane. Thus, in turn creates a higher ball track. As the semi roller has been identified as the most effective, lets explore the possibility of changing a spinner release to a semi roller.

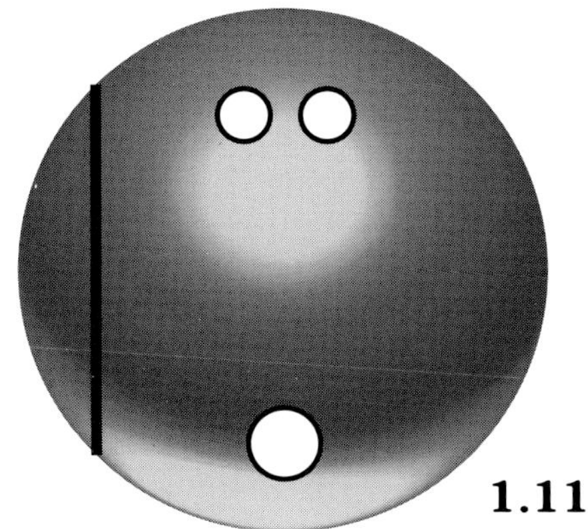
1.11

**Spinner Roll Ball Track**

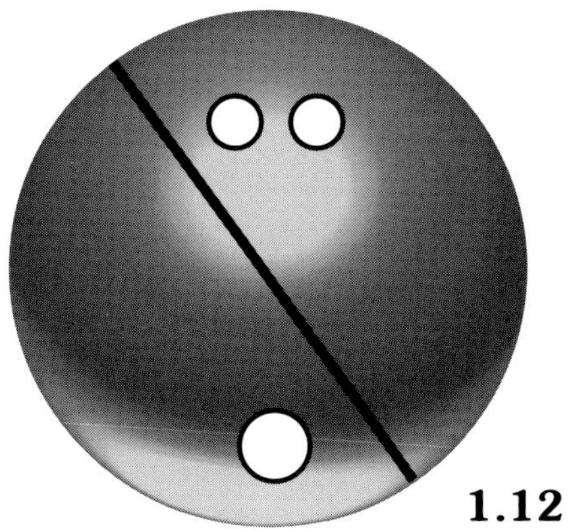
1.12

**Full Roller Ball Track**

The one main element that must first be addressed is the physical position of the bowler. As mentioned earlier in the example of increasing revolutions, the bowler must be in a strong biomechanical position, with the bowling arm and hand also in a favorable position. Once this is achieved, we can make adjustments to the grip to bring the ball track closer to the fingers and thumb.

The easiest way to change the spinner roll is to change the finger and thumb pitches. Two elements of a spinners release are early or excessive "turning" at the point of release, or late release of the fingers and thumb. Based on the knowledge gained through this chapter, the following changes would be recommended.

**Less lateral pitch - as given in the previous example to decrease rotation**

**Increased reverse pitch in the fingers and thumb**

As a reminder, we must make these changes in moderation, and stay within the 1/8 - 1/4 of an inch parameters of our base grip. However, once these factors have been attended to, the bowler should feel less "turn" at the bottom of the swing, and an earlier release. Thus raising the ball track to a more desirable position.

## FULL ROLLER

The full roller was a very popular roll during the 1960's and 1970's when lacquer was used as the lane finish. The full rollers track ran between the finger and thumb holes (figure 1.12), and covered the greatest amount of the balls surface as possible. This release allowed the bowler to have good control over the balls reaction, with only a small backend hook. However, as lane surfaces and bowling balls have changed, the full roller track has become less effective.

The full roller is a little different from the spinner, in terms of making adjustments to the grip to alter the roll. Although some adjustments can be make, the majority of change has to come from the bowler. The bowler has to adjust to a new motion at the bottom of the swing and during the release. Therefore, it is most beneficial to practice with a ball which has been drilled with the bowlers "base grip" and work with a certified instructor to insure proper change for this portion of their bowling game.

# CONCLUSIONS

It is important to remember that bowling ball fitting is an ART not a SCIENCE!
What this means is that you may encounter a certain "trial and error" period before you decide upon the correct grip for you. Then, once you have found this "perfect" grip, it is very possible it can change as your bowling career advances.

Many of the high average amateur and professional players make grip changes as they become more versatile players. Each time they alter their game where it effects their timing, armswing, or release, quite often this will also mean a grip change.

The message is patience! A good Pro Shop ball fitter will get you "close" on the first time you are fit. Just remember, you may have to make small adjustments to "fine tune" the grip to your game.

# Chapter 2

## HOW MUCH DOES THAT NEW BALL HOOK?

This has to be the most common question asked, when a bowler is shopping for a new ball. The old ball does not hook enough any more, and they are looking for a new ball that will give them more hook and better scores. I would venture to guess that this has been the conversation between pro shop operators and bowling customers in Pro Shops throughout the world for many years.

What must be understood, is that all bowling balls have a potential to hook. Some have a greater potential than others based on their surface and core design (which will be explained later). However, they all have the potential to hook. The deciding factor for how much the ball will hook largely depends on the bowler that is throwing the ball. Is the bowler a Hook Ball Player or a Straight Player? How fast or slow is the ball being thrown? How many revolutions does the Player generate? What is the lane condition they are bowling on? All of these questions must be taken into consideration when attempting to analyze how much the ball will hook for a certain bowler.

With strict consideration to the bowling ball, the main factors that will dictate the balls hook potential are;

Bowling Ball Surface
Core/Weight Block design
Balance

In this chapter we will be discussing the bowling ball surface, and how to alter the surface for your specific type of game. In the following chapters we will address the inside design of the ball, and how to balance the ball for a specific reaction. But first, lets take a quick look back into history and observe the evolution of bowling balls based on their surface.

# THE EVOLUTION OF THE BOWLING BALL COVER

## HARD RUBBER

When bowling was in its heyday, back in the 1950's and 1960's, bowlers were competing on a fairly soft finish of either shellac or lacquer. Because this lane surface was softer, bowlers needed a ball with a harder cover for effective control and scoring. During this time period, the ball most commonly used was a hard rubber bowling ball.

As time progressed to the 1960's and 70's two major changes began to take place. One involved the lane surface. The other involved experimentation with the cover of the bowling ball. The major change with the lane surface came in the form of a new harder finish, called the urethane finish. The previous lacquer finish was being discouraged by insurance companies because of its flammable material. The new product, urethane, proved to be a finish which is less flammable, and easier to maintain.

The main factor between the lacquer finish and the new urethane finish as far as the bowlers were concerned, was in the reaction of their ball as it rolled down the lane. On the previously soft finish of lacquer, hard rubber balls would hook, and work well with that surface. However, with the new urethane surface, the hard rubber balls would hook considerably less. The reason being that the urethane surface was much harder, and when matched with a hard rubber bowling ball more skid was produced which equalled less hook.

## POLYESTER

The second change came in the way of the cover of the bowling ball. Due to the hard rubber surface, bowling balls only came in one color, Black. Upon researching "colored" bowling balls, manufacturers realized that a new cover material would need to be used. They found that polyester could be molded to produce bowling balls, which also allowed color to be introduced into the finished product.

In addition, they discovered that different pigments used to color the balls would make the ball either harder or softer. Furthermore, upon testing these balls, they discovered that the softer balls would hook considerably more than the harder balls. Hence, bowling ball manufacturers began to experiment with various materials to allow the ball a chance to "change directions" or hook as it rolled down the lane.

It was also during this time that bowling balls were "Soaked" to produce more hooking power as the ball rolled down the lane. The now famous Don McCune was credited as the first bowler to alter the surface of the ball with chemicals, having the intent to make the cover of the ball softer and produce more hook. As the well documented story goes, Don went on to win 6 titles that year on the PBA Tour and really "opened the eyes" of fellow bowlers and manufacturers as to what could be done with the cover of the ball.

The problem with the soakers was twofold. First, the cover of the balls were so soft, that they damaged the finish on the front part of the lanes. This made lane maintenance very difficult for bowling centers, and lessened the life of their lanes. The second problem was with the chemicals used to soak these balls. The chemicals were highly flammable, and unsafe.

Finally, the PBA stepped forward and realized that this was a problem with which needed to be dealt. They discovered a device called a durometer, which could measure the hardness of the outside of the bowling ball. Upon testing the chemically treated balls, they made a significant discovery. The soaked bowling balls would have a durometer reading of 30 - 50 on the device, and balls which were not soaked would have readings of 75 - 90. A very big difference!

Based on their findings, the PBA enacted the rule that a bowling ball must have a minimum hardness of 75 based on the durometer readings. Any ball tested below 75 would not be allowed for use in any PBA competition. Soon after, the American Bowling Congress enacted a rule stating all bowling balls used in ABC sanctioned competition must have a minimum hardness of 72. Both of these rules still hold true today.

Now the parameters were set. Bowling manufacturers could develop bowling balls that hooked, but had to meet the new rules for hardness.

## SOFT RUBBER

As you can imagine, manufacturers were now busy researching and developing balls that would both hook and meet the new criteria for hardness. The most significant cover introduced after this ruling was the soft rubber cover. As opposed to the previously mentioned hard rubber ball, the soft rubber ball would give the bowler the chance for the ball to change directions or hook considerably more as it rolled down the lane.

The only drawback to the soft rubber ball is that it would absorb oil quite rapidly, and as a result dry the front part of the lane (the heads) very quickly. Consequently, bowlers would have to make adjustments more quickly than usual as the lanes would change as the conditioner was absorbed.

## URETHANE

One of the most revolutionary changes in the cover of the ball occurred during the late 1970's and early 1980's. This was the advent of the urethane cover.

The urethane bowling ball had a few unique characteristics.

1. Harder cover for more durability
2. Surface could be changed for greater diversity
3. Better carry power

The harder cover proved much more durable and longer lasting than either the polyester or soft rubber bowling balls. This was greatly appreciated by the bowling consumers as they had been dealing with bowling balls which cracked around the fingers, or generally were gouged by the machines and ball returns.

Surface alterations were now more popular as bowlers tried to use their urethane ball on all types of lane conditions. Changing the surface of the ball had been done for quite a long time, however, now it was more common as bowlers discovered they could make their ball react differently by altering the surface of their ball.

Finally, higher average bowlers could realize better carry when using the new urethane balls. The reason being that the urethane balls would grab the lanes and hook stronger on the backends therefore carrying the 5 pins and breaking up the bucket leaves which had been previously left. Thus scoring was higher for the more skillful players.

## REACTIVE RESIN

It seems that every decade has seen a new bowling ball cover come onto the market. In the 1960's it was Hard Rubber, in the 1970's it was Polyester, the 1980's witnessed the advent of Urethane, and now for the 90's we have a new coverstock known as Reactive Resin.

Just as the other coverstocks made a significant change in the game, reactive resin has done the same. This revolutionary coverstock has increased averages from the amateur to professional ranks, and has helped to rejuvenate our sport.

Reactive resin bowling balls perform differently from other balls as a result of 2 important factors.

1.) Resin balls are "Tacky" to the touch, which produces better traction or gripping power as the ball rolls down the lane.

2.) Resin balls, when polished, store their energy through the front part of the lane, which leaves the hooking potential of the ball for the backends. This creates a very powerful backend reaction, as compared to traditional urethane.

Understanding the use of energy, in terms of ball reaction, will help to differentiate urethane and reactive resin ball reaction.

## STORED ENERGY

The terms "stored energy" or "utilized energy" refers to the reaction of the ball as it skids or rolls down the lane.

Reactive resin and urethane bowling balls, when polished, both store energy as they roll through the front portion of the lane (figure 2.1 on next page).

This is accomplished due to the polish used on the cover of the ball. The polish decreases the traction which the ball has when dull, and allows the ball to skid.


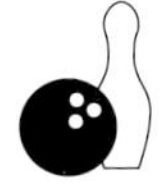

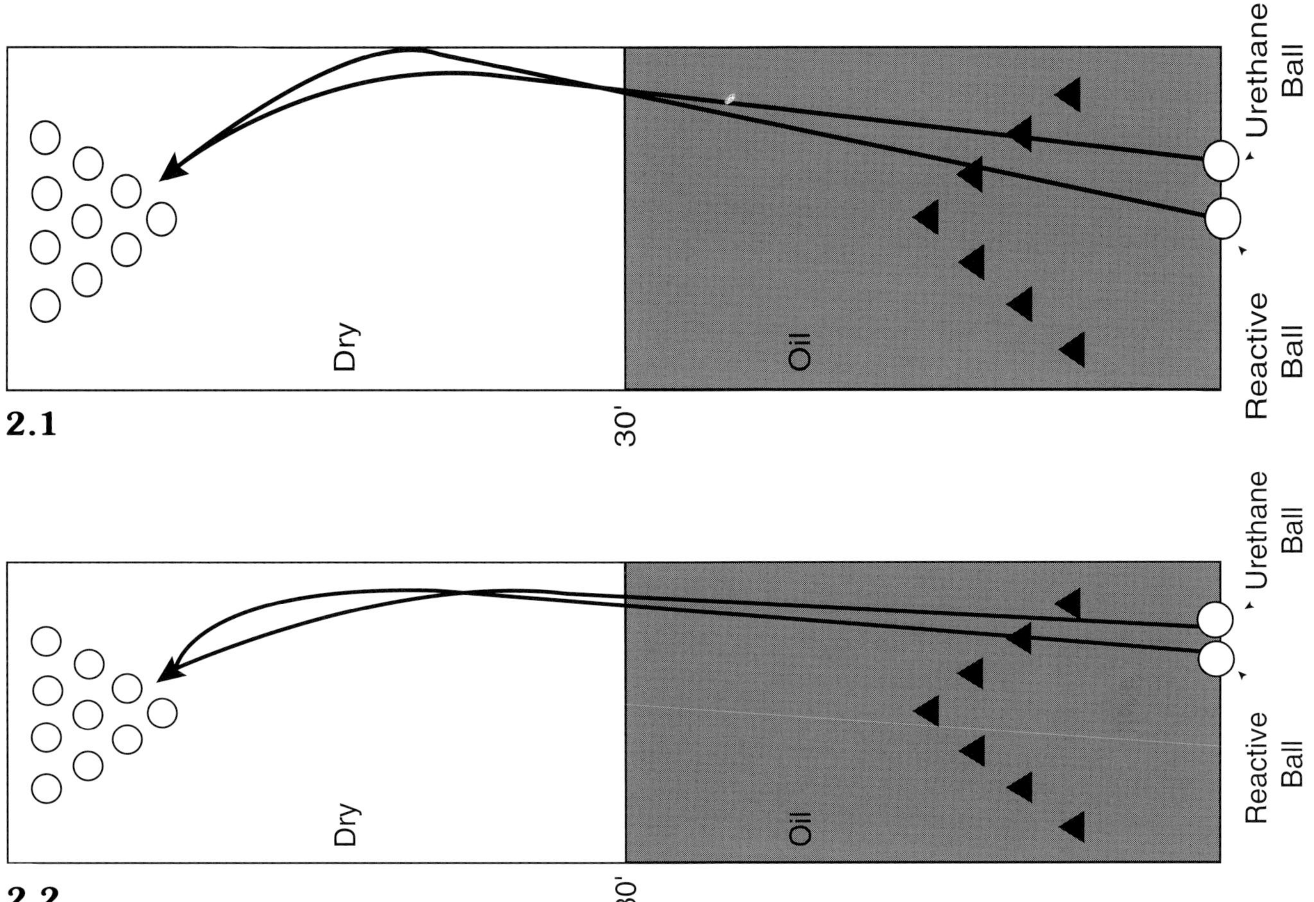


However, the reaction characteristics are quite different in the backend of the lane. Here, on a medium oiled lane condition, the urethane ball will begin to roll and hook moderately as there is an is increased friction due to less oil on the backend portion of the lane.

Conversely, the resin ball on the same lane condition will grip the lane stronger on the backends due to the tacky cover, and once again the increased friction. Thus the reaction produced will be much stronger than traditional urethane.

The difference between urethane and reactive resin balls becomes less when they both have a dull surface, as opposed to a polished surface. Once again using a medium oiled lane condition, both the urethane and resin balls will begin to roll earlier due to the increased friction caused by the duller surface. Therefore, as the balls begin to roll earlier, they use a portion of their energy early, leaving less energy for the backends (figure2.2).

Less energy saved for backend reaction will result in less hook potential, and less backend reaction. For very heavily oiled lane conditions, a dull urethane ball would quite possibly still be the ball of choice.

The final difference between urethane and reactive resin comes in the "hitting" power of these two balls. As previously stated, resin balls provide better gripping power on the backends, and produce greater hooking potential on the backends. This greater hooking potential usually translates into better hitting power and ultimately better carry. Therefore, the by-product of the tremendous backend reaction, when controlled, is much higher scoring with reactive resin balls.

## CONCLUSIONS

Reactive Resins are the coverstock of the 1990's. How long will they last, or when will a new surface be introduced? This is anyone's guess. However, there is no doubt that Reactive Resin bowling balls are here to stay.

The important key to understand is that other coverstocks, such as Urethane and Polyester, should still be used when the conditions are suitable. In later chapters, we will study how certain bowlers can use these surfaces to control their ball reaction, when Reactive Resins overreact.

Now that we understand how coverstocks have evolved, lets explore how the surface of the ball can be altered to provide specific reactions on various lane conditions.

# Customizing the Ball Surface

As we stated in the previous chapter, bowlers truly began to experiment with altering the ball surface when the urethane finish was introduced. The higher average players understood the advantage the urethane cover gave them, and tried to utilize the ball on as many different conditions as possible.

This is even more relevant today with the advent of the reactive resin bowling balls. The tremendous hooking and carry power tempt us to use this ball as often as possible, to maximize our scoring potential. However, there are still occasions where a traditional urethane or even polyester ball can still be the optimal weapon of choice. Therefore, for today's equipment and conditions, we must understand how to customize the cover of the ball to our personal style and the lane condition on which we are competing.

Once again you must take into consideration what type of bowler you are. The Hook Ball Player will alter the ball surface for a particular reaction (usually for more skid) while the Stroker Player will adjust the surface in a different manner. The important factor is to identify your style and make the necessary adjustments. In this chapter we will identify which surfaces are better for both types of players to hopefully clarify which is best for you.

## WHY SHOULD YOU CHANGE THE BALL SURFACE?

One of the most important points in understanding ball reaction is to understand that changing the surface of the ball is the easiest and usually most effective way to change ball reaction. Using a different surface, a ball with a different coverstock (Reactive Resin, Urethane, Polyester, etc.) or changing the surface of the existing ball, can alter the ball reaction tremendously. As we have previously covered the different types of coverstock, lets take a closer look at altering the cover of the ball we are using.

When a new ball is delivered to the pro shop it comes in either 1 of 2 states, polished or dull. Both conditions will make the ball react in a specific manner. First, lets take a look at the dull cover.

# DULL SURFACE

The last step in the manufacturing process is the preparation of the surface of the ball. When the ball is to be left in a dull state, the manufacturer will usually finish the ball by sanding it to a predetermined finish. The range of sanding is between 200 to 600 grit depending on the product and the desired result. The norm is somewhere around 320. But what do all these grits and numbers mean? Lets look at the following example.

If you have ever "felt" sandpaper, you know that the lower number the grit the more coarse and abrasive the sandpaper. Hence the more abrasive the sandpaper, the deeper the "ridges" are when applied to the surface of the ball. Therefore, by sanding a bowling ball with 200 grit sandpaper you will create far deeper ridges than when using 600 grit sandpaper (figure 3.1).

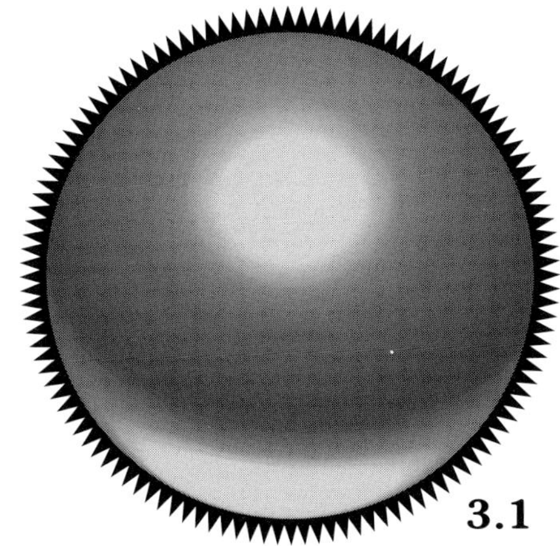


**Simulated Ball Cover with 200 Grit Finish**

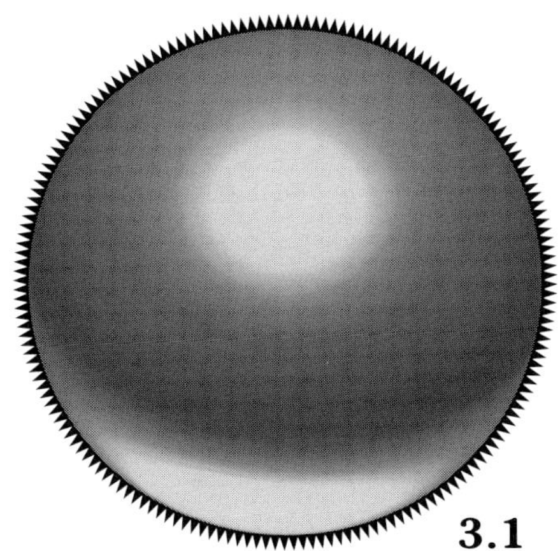


**Simulated Ball Cover with 600 Grit Finish**

How all of this relates to ball reaction is by looking at the aforementioned "ridges" that this sanding creates. The ridges can be equated to an automobile tire. The deeper the ridges, the more it is like an auto tire with deep treads for traction. For the auto tire, the deeper treads result in more traction on wet or icy pavement. In the case of our bowling ball, the deep ridges result in an earlier roll on a heavily oiled lane condition.

Therefore, it should be easy to conclude that a ball which has been finished with 200 grit will begin to roll much earlier than a ball finished with 600 grit. In comparison, the 600 grit finish will cause the ball to initially skid longer than the 200 grit finish. Obviously there are grits which fall in between these, and will affect the cover and reaction based on how coarse or smooth they are.

One of the major problems bowlers face after the purchase of a new ball is that after a certain amount of time and usage, the ball generally does not hook as much as when it was brand new. This occurs because the ball "picks up" oil and dirt each time it is rolled down the lane. Eventually, the ridges created by the sanding become filled with this oil and dirt, and ultimately the ball loses "traction."

An easier way to understand this is to relate back to our analogy of the auto tire. When the tire is new, the tread is fresh and the traction is very good. However, after a certain amount of usage the tread will begin to wear off of the tire, and if used too long the tire will become "bald." At this point, when the tire is used on a wet or icy condition it will react differently from a new tire. It will slip and spin on the ice and not provide any traction.

The same is true of a bowling ball which has been used for a certain number of games. The oil and dirt become packed into the ridges of the surface, and greatly diminish the gripping power of the ball. This is especially true with today's reactive resin balls as these balls pick up dirt much easier than conventional urethane balls. Ultimately the ball tends to skid much longer than when originally purchased.

There are two solutions to overcoming this problem. The first solution covers all types of bowling balls to keep them dull, while the second is primarily used for reactive resins.

## SOLUTION #1

The most effective way to keep a bowling ball dull is to wash it. That's right, you can wash you bowling ball to remove the dirt and oil and restore an almost new finish to the surface. The key to this solution is that you wash the ball every 15 - 20 games starting from when the ball is new. By limiting this number of games to the balls surface, the oil and dirt will not be packed into the ridges too deeply, and can still be removed. However, if you try this on an old ball, or a ball with many games on it, the result will not be as good.

There are most likely skeptics that say this will not help, but here is a quick story to defend this process.

LPBT Champion and Team USA coach Jeri Edwards attributes her Greater Atlanta Open crown to the fact that she washed her bowling ball each night during the tournament. According to Jeri, the lane condition was very long oil with little backend hook. Therefore, it was very important that she had the ball rolling early to insure a slight hook before the ball hit the pins. The ball she used had the right balance for the condition, however she needed to keep the surface clean for maximum hooking potential. Therefore, each night during the tournament, Jeri would take the ball back to her hotel and wash it for the next days competition. The end result Jeris' knowledge of how to control the ball surface, combined with a little extra work each evening, helped her to win the tournament.

The process for washing the ball is as follows:

Step 1 — Cover the finger and thumb holes with black tape, to prevent water from damaging any tape in these holes.

Step 2 — Fill the sink 1/2 way with warm water and a grease cutting detergent (Usually a dishwashing detergent that cuts grease will do)

Step 3 Using a sponge or towel (nothing abrasive) wash the ball until you are satisfied with the condition of the cover.

Step 4 Let the ball dry and go bowling!

### SOLUTION #2

This solution is for reactive resin balls which pick up dirt and belt burns after a short period of usage. Many companies have now introduced products that can clean the cover of reactive balls with little difficulty. I recommend using these products, or having the pro shop clean the ball for a small fee.

Just as the oil and dirt affect the reaction of the urethane balls, the same can be said for belt burns and dirt on reactive resins. Eventually, if the ball is not cleaned, these will create less traction for the ball, and ultimately less hook.

The important key to remember is that cleaning the ball with either these products, acetone or alcohol only cleans the surface of the ball. The oil and dirt built up within the ridges of the cover and cannot be removed by these products. That is why you see bowlers use alcohol to clean their ball, which does make the ball hook more for 2 or 3 shots, then it is back to going straighter. Washing is still the only way to truly restore the surface.

## MEDIUM SURFACE

As mentioned in the previous section, a bowling ball with more than 20 - 30 games will begin to go straighter due to the oil and dirt filling the ridges on the surface, and decreasing the balls traction (figure 3.2). The cleaning process was covered to explain how a new ball can be kept fresh for heavy oil conditions. However, the ball with 30, 50, or 100 games can also be a very useful weapon. A ball of this nature is called a medium surface ball.

**Medium Surface Ball after 30 or more games**

### CHARACTERISTICS OF THE MEDIUM SURFACE

This ball has never been washed and never been polished. However, over the aforementioned number of games the ball has picked up a slight shine due to the oil and dirt collecting in the cover.


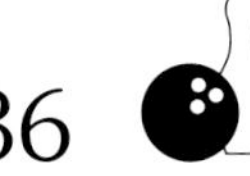

As most people have a "Favorite" ball, the medium surface ball would fall into this category. The bowler has usually had the ball for 1/2 of a season or longer and has become accustomed to its reaction.

This ball is most often recommended as a test ball when encountering new lane conditions, most commonly during tournaments. This ball is used because the bowler understands how the ball should react under "normal" conditions and can make adjustments to a more dull or shiny cover based on the results of the test throws.

Finally, if a bowler has only 1 ball, than hopefully it will fall into this category, as it would be most versatile over a variety of lane conditions.

As the washed ball would be best suited for a heavier oil condition, the medium surface ball could be used on the following conditions:

1.) Medium to Oily lanes
2.) Medium Oiled lanes
3.) Medium to Dry lanes

As lane conditions change, and they always do, the medium surface ball is the natural progression from the washed ball. For example;

A bowler starts a tournament on fairly heavily oiled lanes, and uses the washed ball to overcome the oil. After a few games, the oil either becomes absorbed into the surface (if playing on wood) or gets carried down or picked up on the surface of the ball. In any of these cases the lane begins to hook more.

Before long, the bowler finds that the washed ball is no longer controllable, and needs a ball to skid further before it hooks. By changing to another ball with a medium surface, the bowler can once again find a controllable and predicable roll, and hopefully continue scoring well until another ball change is needed.

# SHINY SURFACE

There are three common means to acquire a shiny surface on the bowling ball They are as follows;

1.) Purchase a factory shined ball from your pro shop
2.) Place your dull or medium surface ball into a ball polishing machine
3.) Ask you pro shop to polish the ball using smooth grades of sandpaper and polishing agents to obtain a ball with maximum skid

## FACTORY SHINED

Many bowling manufacturers now introduce bowling balls which already have a shiny surface. This is especially true of today's reactive resin balls.

To obtain this factory shined surface, the manufacturers literally put the balls through a machine which is similar to a large ball polishing machine. Before they enter the polishing area, they are still in a dull state, which therefore means they still have the previously described "ridges" on their surface. However, by placing the balls into the polishing machine, they become shiny as wax is applied to the surface of the ball, and then buffed to a very high gloss.

In this process, the wax acts like the oil and dirt in the previous example of the medium surface ball. The wax fills the ridges on the surface of the ball, and reduces the balls traction, thus producing skid (figure 3.3).

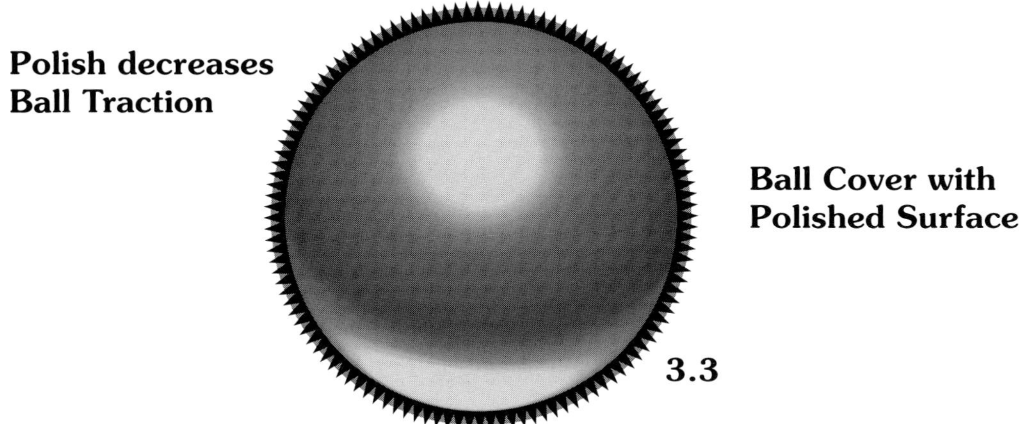


**3.3**

However, many of the new bowling balls are still finished with a dull surface. If this is the case, and you wish to use the new ball for medium to dry lane conditions, simply use either of the following two methods to obtained your desired result.

## BALL POLISHING MACHINE

Before we understand how these machines work, we must first understand this simple concept, **All ball polishing machines are not consistently maintained!** This is unfortunate, as a well maintained ball polishing machine can earn its owner a tidy profit, not to mentioned serving bowlers well when the lanes become dry!

Keeping that in mind, a good ball polishing machine can be very useful. The concept of the machine is simple, and almost the same as the process described in the factory shined process. Wax is applied to the surface of the ball, and buffed into the ridges to make the ball shiny and reduce the amount of the balls traction. The advantage with this machine is that we can determine how polished we want the ball to be.

On most machines, there are three or four options for how long the ball is in the machine. Obviously, the longer the ball is in the machine the more polished it will become. Therefore, if you only want a small gloss on the surface (for slightly more skid) than you would choose the quickest cycle. If you need maximum skid, the longest cycle would be the best choice.

** It is important to note there are a variety of machines now used in bowling centers. Some polish the bowling ball, as previously mentioned, while others merely clean the surface without applying wax. Therefore, be certain which machine is present in the bowling center.*

## ULTRA POLISHING FOR MAXIMUM SKID

This is a process which has evolved over a number of years and has now become very popular with the reactive resin balls. This process not only involves polishing the surface of the ball for reduced traction, but also removing the ridges on the surface for the smoothest surface possible!

As this will take usually 20 - 30 minutes per ball, the pro shop will most likely charge a fee for the work. However, it becomes a nominal fee when compared to the benefits you can receive when the lanes become very dry.

If the process begins with a dull ball, the following sequence of steps must be followed for the best results.

First, this process must be done with the use of a ball spinner. The spinner insures that the sanding will be done evenly, leaving no unwanted "flat spots."

Next, the process calls for sanding the ball in a similar manner as to when a ball is resurfaced. This means that one grade of sandpaper is used across the entire ball before moving onto the next grade. The easiest way to accomplish this is to use the following method;

Step 1) Place the ball in the ball spinner with the grip lying along the right side of the spinner, leaving the left side of the ball (from the grip) facing up.
* Sand the ball for approximately 30 seconds to 1 minute in this position

Step 2) Move the ball so the grip is lying along the left side of the spinner leaving the right side of the ball (from the grip) facing up.
* Sand the ball for approximately 30 seconds to 1 minute in this position

Step 3) Move the ball so the grip is facing up in the ball spinner
* Sand the ball for approximately 30 seconds to 1 minute in this position

Step 4) Move the ball so the grip is facing the bottom of the spinner (Opposite of the grip facing up) * Sand the ball for approximately 30 seconds to 1 minute in this position

By using this procedure, the ball will be sanded completely and evenly.

As we mentioned at the beginning of this chapter, a new ball is usually finished with 320 grit sandpaper. If this is the case, and we want to make this dull ball shiny, we would use the previously mentioned procedure while applying the following sequence of sanding;

400 grit
600 grit
800 grit
1,000 grit
1,200 grit
2,000 grit

In effect, each time you use a smoother grade (higher number) of sandpaper, you are removing a layer of the deep ridges that the original sanding created. In doing this, you are making the surface smoother which will ultimately result in less traction and greater skid than any of the previously mentioned methods (figure 3.4).

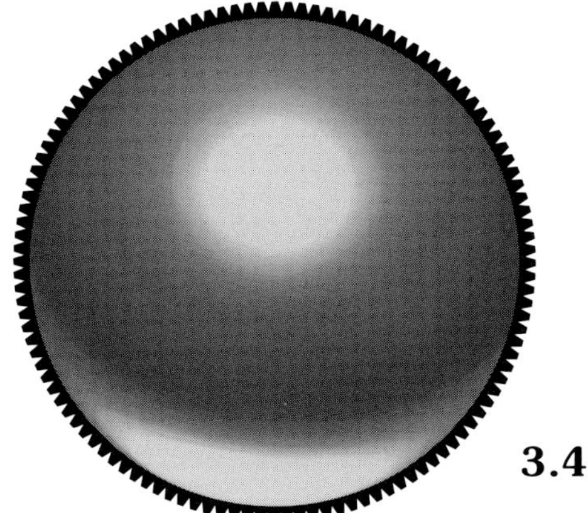

**Ball Cover with Minimal Traction or Gripping Power**

**3.4**

After this sanding process has been completed, a polishing compound is applied to make the ball as shiny as possible. The end result - maximum skid!!

It is important to note that this process can be altered based on the desired reaction. For example;

A Stroker Player needs to create more skid than just using the ball polishing machine, however does not need the maximum skid of sanding the ball to 2,000. The solution would be to sand the ball to a 600 or 800 finish and then polish the ball. This will still leave a minimal amount of traction for ball reaction, combined with the shiny surface needed for initial skid.

## ALTERING THE REACTIVE RESIN SURFACE

Any bowler, who has used a reactive resin bowling ball, knows that there is a sizable difference in ball reaction, when compared to traditional urethane bowling balls. The same is true when the surface of each is altered.

### DULL FINISH

When a reactive resin ball is dull, its reaction is fairly similar to a urethane surface in the same dull state. The reason being that each ball will initiate an early roll, as a result of the dull surface. However, the reactive ball will most likely provide a slightly stronger backend reaction

 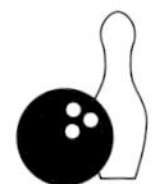

(based on the lane condition) than the urethane ball because of its "Tacky" surface. This surface provides additional traction as the ball reaches the drier boards on the backend of the lane, and therefore provides the added hook.

## POLISHED FINISH

Here is where the major difference occurs. When the urethane ball is polished, its ridges become filled with wax, and its traction reduced. When the same process is completed on a reactive resin ball, its ridges also become filled with wax, reducing its traction. With both surfaces, the polishing process will initially provide longer skid due to the reduced traction.

The difference occurs on the backend of the lane. The urethane ball will generally continue its skid and provide moderate backend reaction. However, the reactive resin ball, upon reaching the dry backends, will hook very sharply by comparison. This is primarily due to the tacky surface, which provides additional traction to the ball on the backends. (As shown in the example on page 31, Chapter 2.)

Both reactions are favorable, when used on the appropriate lane condition. In the following chapters, we will study lane conditions and learn when to use each surface, to gain the best possible reaction.

# TOURNAMENT XYZ

As we have briefly studied the progression from a washed ball to a medium surface ball, lets now look at a common tournament condition, and the process in which a lane "breaks down". This in turn will help us to understand when to use each of these surfaces.

## WHAT TYPE OF BOWLER AM I ?

In the following tournament example, and throughout this book, three styles of bowlers will be used;

Hook Ball Player - Stroker Player - Straight Player

Their games are classified as follows;

Straight Player - A bowler with average to above average ball speed, combined with minimal release action, providing a backend hook of 5 boards or less from the breakpoint.

Stroker Player - A bowler with average or below average ball speed, combined with moderate release action, providing a backend hook of 5 - 10 boards from the breakpoint.

Hook Ball Player - A bowler with average to above average ball speed, combined with a strong release providing a backend hook of 10 boards or more from the breakpoint.

Most bowlers will generally fall into one of these three categories, or be positioned between two of them. For the purpose of explanation in this book, these three categories will be used. Therefore, determine which type of player best suites your game, and substitute yourself for this player in the following examples.

## THE PLAYING FIELD

This wood surface bowling center has maintained their lanes in the following manner for Tournament XYZ;

The lanes have been double oiled to 30 feet, and buffed to 35 feet. (a very common condition). Also the backends have been stripped, and are fresh for this tournament.

*Therefore total oil distance is 35 feet, leaving 25 feet of dry backends to start the tournament.*

## WHAT BALL SHOULD I START WITH?

As the tournament begins, the Hook Ball Players begin with medium to shiny equipment as their game calls for a ball that skids more than that of a Stroker or a Straight Player. If the Hook Ball Player chooses a shiny ball to start with, they will opt for either a factory shined ball or a ball which has been put into a ball polishing machine. This ball will provide skid because of the shiny surface, however will still provide some traction for the backends.

The Stroker Player will most likely choose a medium surface ball, as a washed ball will most likely roll too early, and a shiny ball will skid too far. Based on the Strokers release and ball speed, the medium surface would be the best choice.

The Straight Player will usually choose a washed ball, as their hook is very minimal. They need a surface to help the ball begin to roll to accomplish a small arc as the ball rolls down the lane.

Given the previously stated lane condition, most of the players (right-handed) will target somewhere between the second and third arrows, however, they will all be using the different bowling balls. Given the surface is wood, and the fact that most of the players will be using reactive balls, the ball track (where the majority of players are targeting around 2nd and 3rd arrows) will begin to dry at a fairly quick pace.

After the second game or so, the bowlers will have to begin making adjustments in their targeting to compensate for the changing lane conditions. This will initially be done by moving their feet and their target deeper into the oil to create more skid for their bowling ball. After another few games of changing their angle on the lane (or sooner), the bowlers will need to change their bowling ball.

Depending on the severity of the lane condition, (which depends a lot upon the condition of the wood surface and type of oil used) the bowlers will most likely make the following adjustments.

## WHAT ADJUSTMENTS DO I MAKE?

The Hook Ball Player will change to either an extremely polished reactive resin ball or to a shiny urethane bowling ball. The highly polished reactive will help the player to gain extra skid as this ball has very little traction after the sanding process. However, it will still provide backend reaction due to the fact that it is still a reactive ball.

If the conditions have depleted to extremely dry, the Hook Ball Player will be forced to change to either a shiny urethane ball, or even a plastic ball in extreme cases. This will help to maximize the skid for this player, and should help to overcome this condition.

## * ADVANCED VARIABLES FOR HOOK BALL PLAYERS

The Hook Ball Player, if versatile, could also use either of the following two options;

1.) Change to a "Weaker" release which would make the ball skid longer. The benefit is more control combined with the opportunity to use the reactive resin ball and the benefits of its carry power.

2.) Change to a lighter bowling ball to generate more speed. As the new resin balls are designed to react well in lighter weights, this gives the player an advantage by having greater ball speed and the strong roll of the lighter ball.

The Stroker Player would now be able to change to a shiny or highly polished reactive ball, and maintain the skid required to score well on this condition.

The Straight Player could now use either the medium or shiny surface, as they will begin to see more ball reaction due to the drier conditions. In this case, the reactive balls truly become a powerful weapon for the bowlers who can be accurate and keep the ball in the pocket as the conditions become drier.

# CONCLUSIONS

Through this tournament example, you should gain the understanding of changing the balls surface as the lane conditions dictate. Through practice, you will be able to make these decisions quickly, as you notice the change in lane conditions and your ball reaction.

As you now have a better understanding of how to change ball surfaces, it is time to experiment. Most bowlers have a few "old" or "unused" bowling balls in their garage or basement. Now is the time to put them to good use.

Take them to your Pro Shop and change the surfaces. For example, sand and polish a ball for spares or dry lanes. Next, dull a ball with 200 grit too observe how early it will roll. The message is to put your old equipment to good use through experimentation. You will gain valuable knowledge in your testing, and might even resurrect a ball in the process.

# Chapter 4

Until the late 1970's, bowling balls were generally constructed in a similar manner. The construction was deemed a three piece design and included the following elements;

Cover Stock material (Chapter 2)

Filler material

A small "Pancake Shaped" weight block

During the years prior to this period, the majority of experimentation for making the ball hook came in the form of different cover stocks. However, during the late 1970's a major change took place from the standpoint of the inner design of the bowling ball.

Hence the advent of the "Two Piece" core design.

The major differences between the two designs, from a manufacturing standpoint, are as follows;

Position of the weight block in the ball
Size and density of the weight block
The amount of coverstock used

Since the introduction of the two piece design there has been an incredible amount of experimentation from bowling ball manufacturers. The intent has been to design bowling balls with unique core designs for improved dynamics and roll characteristics. Some have been successful others have not been so successful. In this chapter, you will learn the difference between the two and three piece design, and be able to understand the reaction of new bowling balls based on their inner construction.

## WHY SO MANY BOWLING BALLS?

The previous material covered in this book should be somewhat familiar to most bowlers who have been in the sport for a certain amount of time. However, the information included

 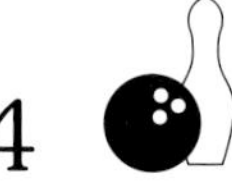

in this chapter, while it has been understood for many years, seems to be constantly changing in the bowling industry.

Not many years ago, ball companies would introduce 1 or maybe 2 new bowling balls in a years time. However, in the last few years, that has changed completely, as it seems ball companies are introducing new balls every few months.

Due to this massive outpouring of new equipment, it has become difficult for pro shops, and especially bowlers, to comprehend all of the new technology on the market. Hopefully, this chapter will enable you to analyze new bowling balls by understanding the fundamentals of core design.

Basically, there are three designs we will study. They are as follows:

1.) Three Piece Weight Block
2.) Two Piece Core Heavy
3.) Two Piece Cover Heavy

These represent the core designs primarily used in today's bowling balls. By understanding how these translate into ball reaction, you can analyze other current and future designs and how they should react.

## A SHORT PHYSICS LESSON

Before we can begin to analyze core design, we must first understand how each of these balls differ. To achieve that, lets first identify the bowlers track and axis points.

**Ball Track** - The area of the ball which comes in contact with the lane surface as the ball rolls down the lane.

* Each ball track is unique based on the bowlers release, and the inner balance of the ball.

**Axis Point** - This is found based on the ball track. Specifically, the axis point is the end of the imaginary line around which the ball rotates as it travels down the lane, and is equidistant from all points of the ball track.

* Once again, as each bowlers ball track is unique to their game, each bowlers axis point is also unique, as it is based on their ball track.

Taking the statement from the definition for axis point, "the point that is equidistant from all areas of the ball track", it would make sense that there would be two such areas on the ball. A point equidistant from the track, to the right side of the track, as well as a point equidistant from the left side of the track.

By connecting these two points, through the center of the ball, we have what is commonly called the axis line. This line (for this demonstration) remains stable as the ball rolls down the lane. Therefore, any weight block design, grip, balance hole, etc. would revolve around this axis line.

A simple test to discover your axis point can be done as follows;

1.) Throw two or three shots in an area on the lane which you know has oil (usually in the middle).
2.) Trace the oil ring or ball track with a grease pencil.
3.) Place the ball on its side keeping the ball track parallel to the surface or table you are using (for a right-handed bowler, simply move the grip to the left until the track becomes parallel with the table).
4.) Using a flexible measuring tape, start at one side of the ball track and measure (by going over the top of the ball) the distance to the other side of the ball track.
5.) Mark the half way point with the grease pencil.
6.) Move the ball 1/4 turn (while still keeping it parallel to the table) and repeat steps 4 and 5 from this different position of the ball track.
7.) Where the two lines meet (where they have crossed from the 1/2 points of the measuring) is you axis point.
8.) Mark the point with a white piece of tape, and throw the ball!

If the ball is balanced in a relatively stable position (which we will cover in the following chapters) you should notice the tape spiraling as the ball rolls down the lane. If this occurs, you have marked the axis correctly. If the tape does not spiral for at least the first 30 - 40 feet of the lane, then repeat the process as you may have incorrectly marked the axis.

Once again, this test helps you to identify your axis point. More importantly, it can also help you to visualize the concept of the weight block revolving around the axis line while as the ball rolls down the lane. Later, we will use the axis point for different purposes in the area of ball balance.

Now that we have identified the ball track and the axis line, lets understand how the two and three piece core designs affect the roll of the ball.

To analyze these two designs, we are going to state that both balls used in this example have the grip drilled over the label.

To begin, lets draw the axis line through the center of each ball. (Diagram 4.0)

 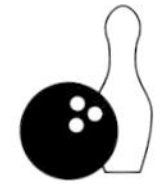

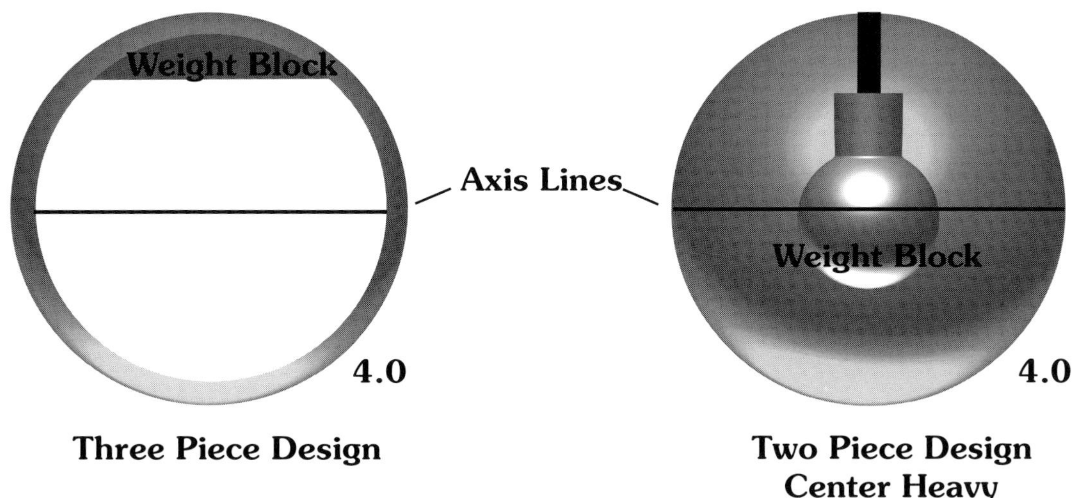


**Three Piece Design**

**Two Piece Design Center Heavy**

Now, lets identify the distance of each weight block in relation to the axis line. Notice that the two piece design has more of its "mass" around the axis line, whereas, the three piece ball has its mass located above the axis line.

The distance of the mass in relation to the axis line gives us the key to understanding how these two balls roll.

As a general rule, the following applies to the overall roll of the ball.

* The closer the mass is to the axis line, the earlier the ball is going to roll while the further the mass is away from the axis line the more the ball will skid.

The following example should help to clarify this concept.

(Hopefully, almost everyone has seen figure skating on television. Therefore, this example should be widely understood.)

As a figure skater begins to spiral in one position, she can only revolve so fast with her arms and one leg extended away from her body. However, if she wants to revolve as fast as possible, she brings her arms and leg close to the rest of her body, and can achieve the fast spiral (figure 4.1). To slow down again, she extends her arms and leg away from her body, and skates away.

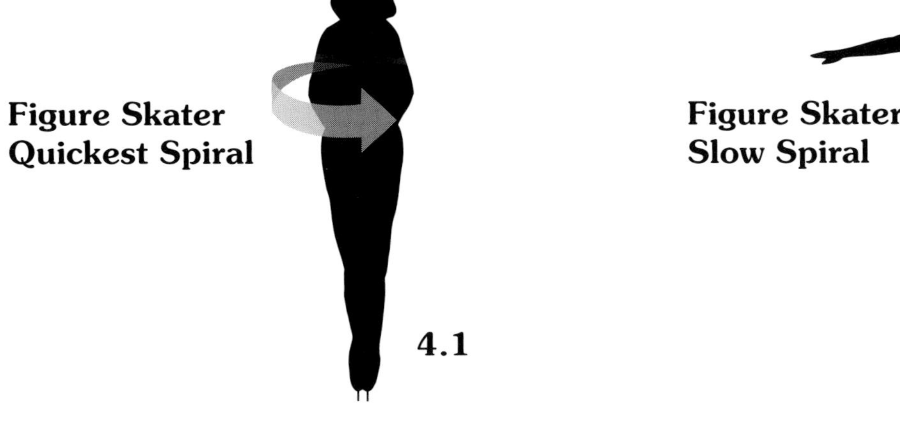


**Figure Skater Quickest Spiral**

**Figure Skater Slow Spiral**

## HOW DOES THIS EXAMPLE RELATE TO THE BOWLING BALL? SIMPLE.

The skaters body represents the axis line when compared to the bowling ball. Her arms and leg represent mass relative to the axis line. When the skaters arms and leg are extended, she cannot spiral very fast. This is very much like a three piece ball as the mass is located away from the axis line (figure 4.2), and consequently takes a long time for the mass to make one revolution around the axis line. Thus the ball, like the skater, cannot revolve very quickly.

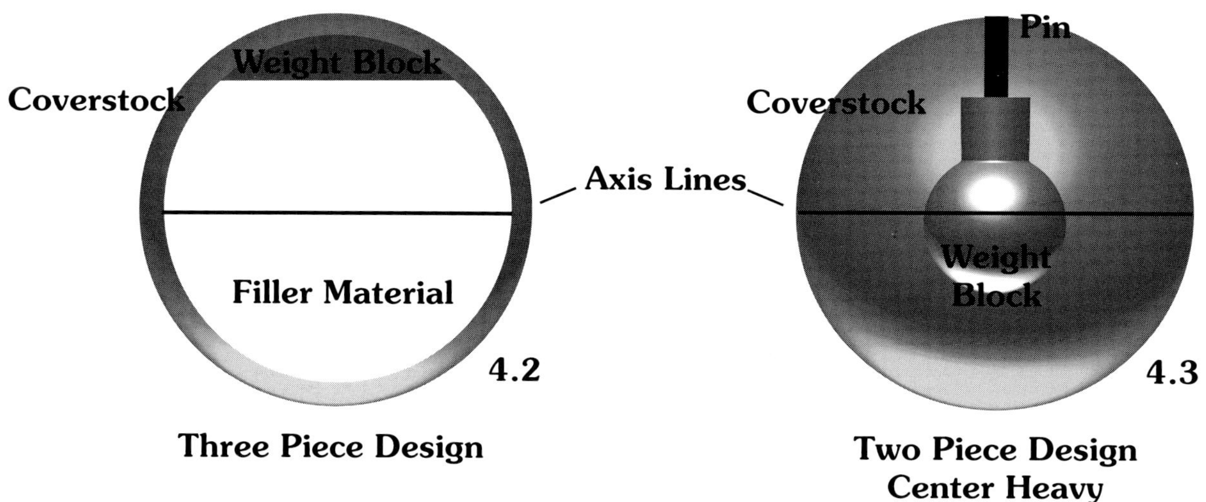


**Three Piece Design**

**Two Piece Design Center Heavy**

The two piece ball is related to the skater in the position where her arms and leg are close to the body. The two piece ball has its mass located around the axis line (figure 4.3), and therefore the mass takes less time to make one revolution around the axis line. Ultimately, this allows the two piece ball to begin rolling much earlier than the three piece ball.

Once you understand this concept of the mass in relation to the axis line, you will go a long way in understanding the roll patterns for many of the balls on the market today and in the future.

## HOW THIS RELATES TO EQUIPMENT OF THE 90'S

When looking at the majority of bowling balls today, their overall characteristics are quite similar to either the two or three piece ball. This is for a specific reason, they work very well!!

As I mentioned earlier, we have seen bowling ball companies experiment with various designs of weightblocks to achieve different reactions. Most of these balls had a short life as they were either too unpredictable, or were not suited for the majority of bowlers. It is for this reason that most of the ball companies have returned, at least for now, to a form of either the two or three piece weightblocks.

The key to understanding any core design, is to identify where the mass is located in relation to the axis line. In the past, and still today, there are many terms used to describe the location of the mass. Here are a few examples;

**Balls with the mass located away from the axis line;**

High Moment of Inertia, High Mass, Shell Heavy, Cover Heavy and High Radius of Gyration

**Balls with the mass located close to or around the axis line;**

Low Moment of Inertia, Low Mass, Center Heavy, Core Heavy and Low Radius of Gyration

Any of these are certainly acceptable terms. The key is to understand how they relate to the inner design of the bowling ball.

As we have identified that the three piece ball has its weight block positioned away from the axis line, we can conclude that it would be considered a Cover Heavy bowling ball.

Likewise, we have identified that a two piece ball has its weight block located around the axis line, and therefore would be considered a Core Heavy or Center Heavy bowling ball.

## WHAT FALLS IN BETWEEN THE TWO AND THREE PIECE BOWLING BALLS?

To this point, we have covered the initial two designs which were mentioned at the beginning of this chapter;

Three piece weight block
and
Two piece core heavy

The third configuration mentioned was the two piece cover heavy weight block. In reality, this is merely a design introduced to have a roll characteristic between the two and three piece designs.

By analyzing the Two Piece Cover Heavy design (figure 4.4), we discover that its mass is both surrounding the axis line and is some distance away from the axis line, covering a larger core area. In some cases, the heaviest portion of this design is located at the top of the weight block. It is for this reason that it gives the ball a roll characteristic between the two previously covered designs.

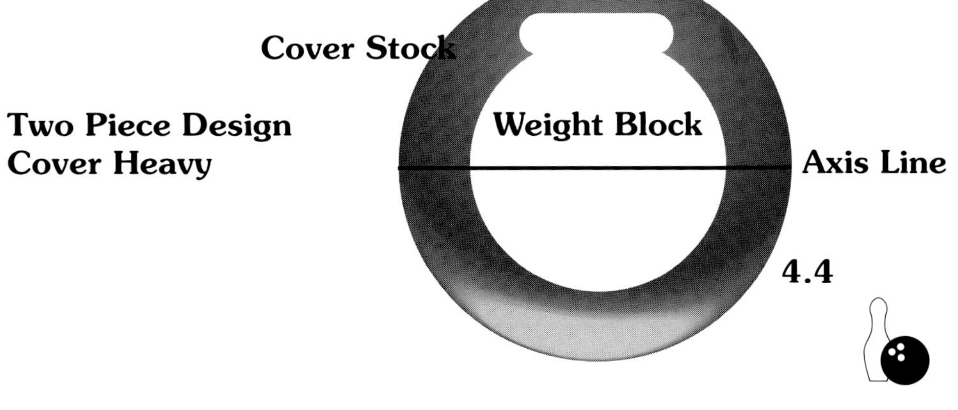

4.4

As this weight block has mass around the axis line, it can be said that this design will roll earlier than the three piece design. The reason being that the three piece ball only has mass located away from the axis line. Therefore, this two piece ball will roll earlier than the three piece design. However, it will not roll as early as the two piece center heavy design.

The difference between the two piece center heavy and the two piece core heavy weight blocks is primarily the position and density of the weightblocks. The center heavy design keeps the majority of its mass around the axis line, where the cover heavy weight block has less mass around the axis, and more mass closer to the cover of the ball. Thus, the two piece center heavy ball will initially begin to roll earlier than the two piece cover heavy ball.

The best way to analyze all three designs is to understand how and when they should be used for different lane conditions.

## MATCHING THE CORE DESIGN TO THE LANE CONDITION

As we have stated, the three piece ball will initially skid the longest of these bowling balls. Therefore, it would only make sense that it would be the best choice for drier lane conditions. Obviously, a dry lane does not require a ball which rolls early, but rather a ball which skids longer and is more controllable for the condition.

Conversely, an oily condition would require a ball which does begin to roll early, to combat the amount of oil on the lane. In this case, the two piece center heavy ball would be the best choice.

The medium condition, not too dry and not too oily, would most likely be suited for the two piece cover heavy ball. As stated, this ball has a roll characteristic between the two previously mentioned, and is best suited for lanes conditioned in this manner.

To go one step further, lets match the type of surface with the weight block design for these conditions;

| | |
|---|---|
| Dry Lanes | Polished cover (either reactive or urethane based on the bowler)<br>Three piece ball for maximum skid and control |
| Medium Lanes | Medium Cover (usually a reactive ball with the cover finished to the needs of the bowler)<br>Two Piece Cover Heavy for medium hook on this condition |
| Oily Lanes | Dull Cover (Once again depending on the bowler)<br>Two Piece Center heavy for early roll on this heavy oil condition |

This should begin to give you an idea of how all of these elements come together in choosing the right ball, for the specific condition upon which you are bowling.

# CONCLUSIONS

Since the mid 1980's we have witnessed weight block designs evolve. As mentioned earlier, the good designs are still being used while the others have been discontinued. Most likely, this is a process which will continue.

Remember, the important factor in analyzing a new weight block design is to determine the position of the mass. Bowling ball companies have been very helpful in providing half sections of their new products, which can help us to determine how the ball will react. However, if you have any questions in regards to a new balls design, ask you Pro Shop operator for details.

Now that we have the knowledge of a bowling balls inner construction, lets study how to balance these weight blocks. In the following chapters, both Static and Dynamic Balancing will be shown as methods to gain desired ball reactions on a variety of lane conditions.

# Chapter 5

As we now understand how a ball is constructed, we must now learn how to balance our bowling ball for specific reactions. Basically there are two methods of balancing a bowling ball;

Static Balance
and
Dynamic balance

Although these may sound like difficult terms, they are relatively easy to understand.

**Static Balance** - Simply means balancing a ball while it is at rest (no movement).

**Dynamic Balance** - Determining the balance while the ball is in motion.

In this chapter we will discuss how to balance a ball statically, and understand how these static weights effect the way the ball rolls down the lane. In the following chapter we will address dynamic balancing.

You may be asking what or how we have derived the term static weights? Quite simply, the scale used to balance a ball while at rest (for industrial purposes) is called a Static Beam Balance. Therefore, the measurements or weights derived from the scale are commonly referred to as static weights. More commonly they are understood as the following;

Top Weight - Bottom Weight
Thumb Weight - Finger Weight
Right Side Weight - Left Side Weight

## UNDERSTANDING STATIC WEIGHTS

As most all bowlers understand, there limits to the amount of static balance which can be used when balancing a ball. The following rules have been enacted and are the standards used by the ABC, WIBC, YABA, PBA, LPBT, and FIQ. These are as follows:

| Balance | Maximum allowance |
|---|---|
| Top Weight/ Bottom Weight | 3 ounces |
| Finger Weight/ Thumb Weight | 1 ounce |
| Right/ Left Side Weight | 1 ounce |

These rules were set forth to restrict bowlers from using illegally balanced bowling balls, and gaining an unfair advantage over other players through the use of equipment. However, as will be explained in the following chapter, these weights are not nearly as important as the position and dynamic balance of the weight block in the bowling ball.

When bowling balls used the three piece weight block design exclusively, prior to the 1980's, this method of balancing a ball served a good purpose. This being that all balls had the same inner design, and the weight blocks all were constructed with the same density. As a result, this set of rules worked well to govern the maximum reaction of a bowling ball.

However, with the advent of the two piece ball, and of their various densities and designs, these rules do not in any way limit the amount of ball reaction. These bowling balls have core designs which range in density from 3 - 11 pounds. Therefore, it is most logical that the position of the mass, or majority of the core weight will have a much greater effect on the way the ball rolls than the actual static weights. This dynamic balancing will be covered in greater detail in the next chapter.

Static weights largely determine the ball reaction of three piece bowling balls. As previously mentioned, two piece designs are governed more by the use of dynamic balancing. Therefore, ***this chapter will focus on the three piece design***, as it is most affected through static balancing.

## HOW STATIC WEIGHTS INFLUENCE THE BALL ROLL

Although, as previously stated, dynamic balance is much more important that than static balance. However, static weights will still be covered, as many bowlers still use three piece equipment. Also, the explanation will help in understanding dynamic balance, when it is studied in the following chapter.

## TOP WEIGHT VS. BOTTOM WEIGHT

Lets first analyze each set of weights, starting with Top and Bottom Weights.

Top Weight is used for two specific reasons.

1.) To offset the grip drilled into the bowling ball

2.) To help the ball initially skid down the lane to prevent early hook.

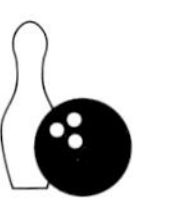

The first of these reasons is quite simple. Every bowlers hand is different, as stated in the first chapter. Some players have large hands, some medium sized, and some small. As a general rule, the larger the hand, the bigger the holes need to be drilled to accommodate the finger and thumb sizes. The bigger the holes, the more weight is taken out of the ball when it is drilled. The Top Weight helps to offset this amount of weight removed when drilling the grip holes. (figure 5.1)

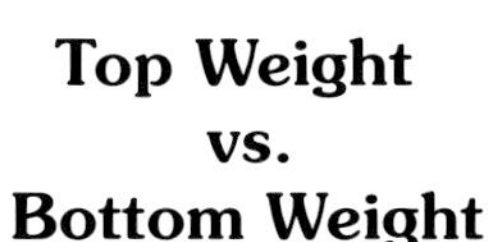


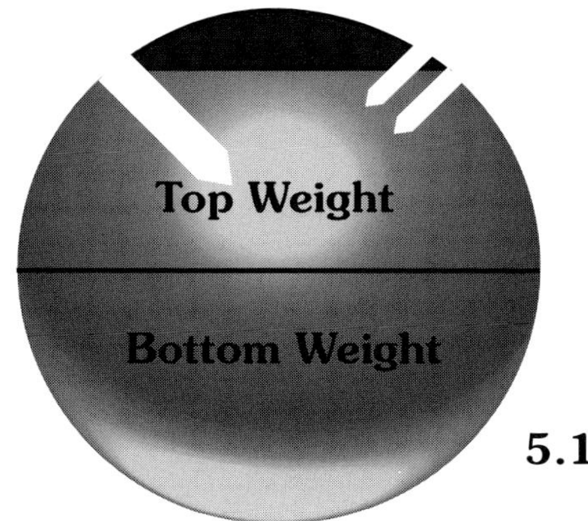


5.1

Due to the varying sizes of grip holes drilled, a larger variance in the amount of Top or Bottom Weight is allowed after drilling for the ball to be legal. Conceivably, there is a 6 ounce range that your ball can fall into after being drilled. This occurs as the rules allow a maximum of 3 ounces of Top Weight or a maximum of 3 ounces of Bottom Weight. After the ball has been drilled, it will fall somewhere in this range. Where it falls, leads us to understanding how it will react.

The second reason for Top Weight is to allow the ball to initially skid as it rolls down the lane. Therefore, the more Top Weight after drilling, the longer the ball will skid (being more prevalent on a three piece design). Conversely, the closer the ball is to Zero Balance, or has Bottom Weight, the earlier it will roll.

Lets look at the following example to determine how these weights influence the ball roll;

* For this example we will assume the bowlers grip removes 2.5 ounces of weight during the process of drilling the grip holes.

| | Ball A | Ball B | Ball C |
|---|---|---|---|
| Top Weight (Before Drilling) | 4.2 OZ | 2.5 OZ | 1.3 OZ |
| Amount of weight removed from grip | 2.5 OZ | 2.5 OZ | 2.5 OZ |
| Net Weight after Drilling | 1.7 OZ (Top Weight) | 0 OZ (Top or Bottom) | 1.2 OZ (Bottom Weight) |

Through this example, we identify Ball A as having the most Top Weight after drilling. Ball B has neither Top or Bottom Weight which is called Zero Balance, and Ball C is the only ball with Bottom Weight after drilling.

Based on these results, the following should hold true in the form of ball reaction, if all other conditions are equal.

Ball A = Maximum skid

Ball B = Medium Skid

Ball C = Earlier Roll

**Once again, previously covered factors such as Coverstock, Surface, and Ball Construction must be considered when comparing these balls.

# RIGHT SIDE VS LEFT SIDE WEIGHT

The easiest way to understand these weights is to first understand where the weight is positioned for each. In figure 5.2, notice that the line drawn through the center of the ball divides the weight equally from left to right. From this diagram, it would be easy to assume that both sides weighed the same if measured on the scale. Therefore, it would be considered to have Zero Balance.

In figure 5.3,, it is clearly shown that the greatest amount of the weight block is positioned on the right side of the ball (when compared to the center line). Therefore, it would be easy to assume that the right side of the ball would weigh more than the left side.

Figure 5.4, indicates that the weight is shifted to the left side of the ball. Based on our previous conclusions, it would be logical to assume that the left side of the ball would weigh more.

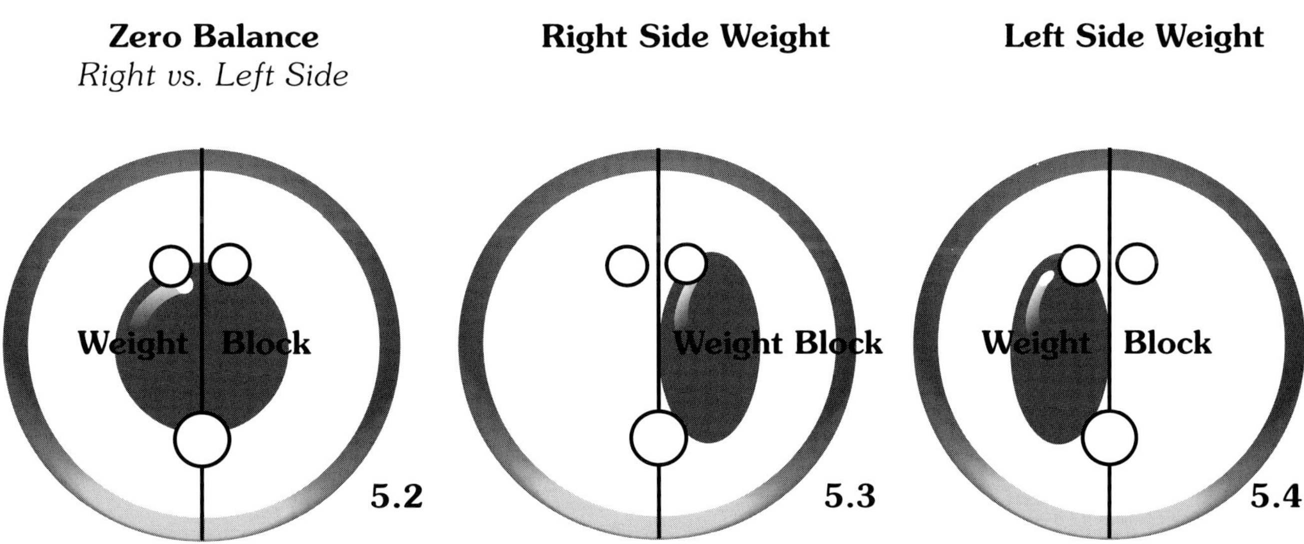

## HOW RIGHT AND LEFT SIDE WEIGHT AFFECT BALL ROLL

*The following reactions may be achieved for a right-handed bowler.*

Right Side Weight = Initial skid, with backend hook.
Zero Balance = Minimal skid, with an even backend reaction.
Left Side Weight = Least initial skid, with minimal backend reaction.

*These reactions may be achieved for a left-handed bowler.*

Left Side Weight = Initial skid with backend hook.
Zero Balance = Minimal skid with an even backend reaction.
Right Side Weight = Least initial skid, with minimal backend reaction.

## RIGHT SIDE WEIGHT

Right Side Weight, for right-handed bowlers is also known as "positive" weight or a "hook" weight. Just the opposite is true for left handers, as Left Side Weight is also referred to in these terms. The reason for these terms is due to the ball reaction they produce as the ball advances towards the pins.

Why does this weight produce more hook than the others? Simply because it is "pulling" the ball towards the pins as it rolls down the lane.

When balancing a ball with Right Side Weight, the right side of the ball has more of the mass positioned (usually) to the right side of the bowlers grip (when looking at the grip in a stable position). However, when the bowler releases the ball, the weight is now in a position facing the left side of the lane, and more importantly facing the pins. Now, the Right Side Weight will contribute to the ball achieving a hook as it rolls down the lane.

The same reaction will take place for a left-handed bowler when using Left Side Weight. The ball will react strongest on the backends in this position, when compared to Zero Balance or Right Side Weight.

## LEFT SIDE WEIGHT

For right-handed bowlers, the opposite of Right Side Weight is Left Side Weight. Just as Right Side Weight will help the ball roll towards the pins and contribute to a "hook," Left Side Weight keeps the mass in a position away from the pins, and allows the ball to achieve less hook as it rolls down the lane.

This balance might initially seem less than desirable for many bowlers, however, it can prove to be a great weapon on certain lane conditions. For example;

A Hook Ball Player is competing on a very dry lane condition. As the lane is providing plenty of hook, the bowler does not need a ball which has been balanced for backend hook.

In this case, a ball with Left Side Weight would be the choice. It will help this bowler to control the lane condition, and keep the ball from overreacting on the backends. Left-handed bowlers would use Right Side Weight in the same manner.

### ZERO BALANCE

Finally, Zero Balance, a ball evenly balanced from left to right, which will produce an even roll as the ball advances towards the pins. In this case, the weight neither favors the right or left side, and produces an even and predictable arc as the ball rolls down the lane.

This reaction can be beneficial on medium to dry lanes, when the bowler needs more backend reaction than Left Side Weight can provide, but not as much as Right Side Weight gives.

In this case, Zero Balance works the same for right and left-handed players.

Once again, the bowlers style (Hook Ball, Stroker, Straight Player), type of coverstock, surface, ball construction, and other static weights will have to be accounted for to derive the exact reaction of any of these weights.

## THUMB VS FINGER WEIGHT

This final category of static weights most relates to the aforementioned Top and Bottom Weights, in terms of ball roll. As we mentioned earlier, Top Weight makes the ball initially skid, while Bottom Weight helps the ball to begin an earlier roll.

Once again, to help in understanding how these weights react, lets look at how they are positioned in the ball.

### FINGER WEIGHT

In figure 5.5, notice that the majority of weight is located closer to the fingers in relationship to the center of grip line. When the ball is weighed, it will show that the fingers side of the ball weighs more than the thumb side. Therefore, when the weight is in this position, it is called Finger Weight.

Similar to Top Weight, Finger Weight helps the ball to maintain a longer skid through the middle portion of the lane. Thus, Finger Weight when combined with Top Weight, will help to achieve a longer skid pattern.

### THUMB WEIGHT

In figure 5.6, we notice that the majority of weight is positioned closest to the thumb. Once again, when the ball is weighed it will show that the thumb portion of the ball is heavier. Therefore when the majority of weight is in this position it is called Thumb Weight. From a ball reaction standpoint, Thumb Weight helps the ball to begin an earlier roll. Therefore, when combined with Bottom Weight, this combination will help the ball to initiate an early roll when dealing strictly with static weights.

## ZERO BALANCE

Just as with Right and Left Side Weight, as well as Top and Bottom Weight, there can be a Zero Balance when dealing with Finger and Thumb Weight. Figure 5.7 indicates that the weight is divided equally between the fingers and thumb, and generally centers around the middle of the grip. Hence, when the ball is weighed in this position, it will be evenly balanced between the fingers and thumb, producing a Zero Balance.

As Finger Weight promotes a longer skid, and Thumb Weight initiates an earlier roll, Zero Balance allows the ball to achieve minimum skid, with an even reaction as it rolls through the middle portion of the lane.

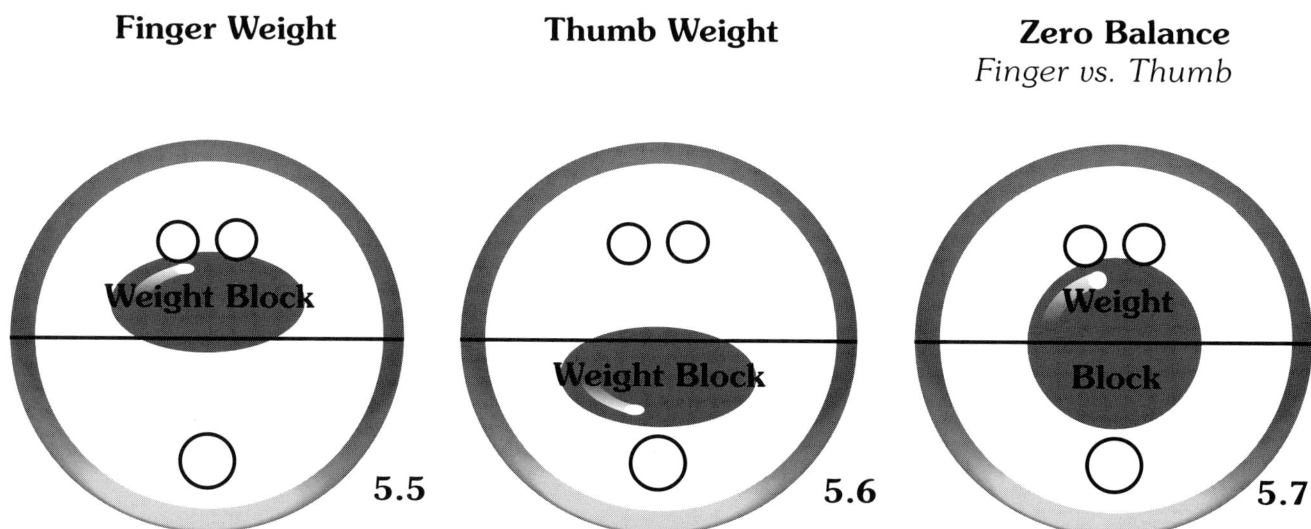


# HOW STATIC WEIGHTS AFFECT BALL ROLL

To this point you should have an understanding of how the previously mentioned static weights relate to ball roll in terms of reaction. Now, lets take a closer look at when these weights have the greatest effect on ball roll in terms of where they react on the lane.

When speaking in terms of the lane, we generally break it down into three areas (figure 5.8);

**5.8**

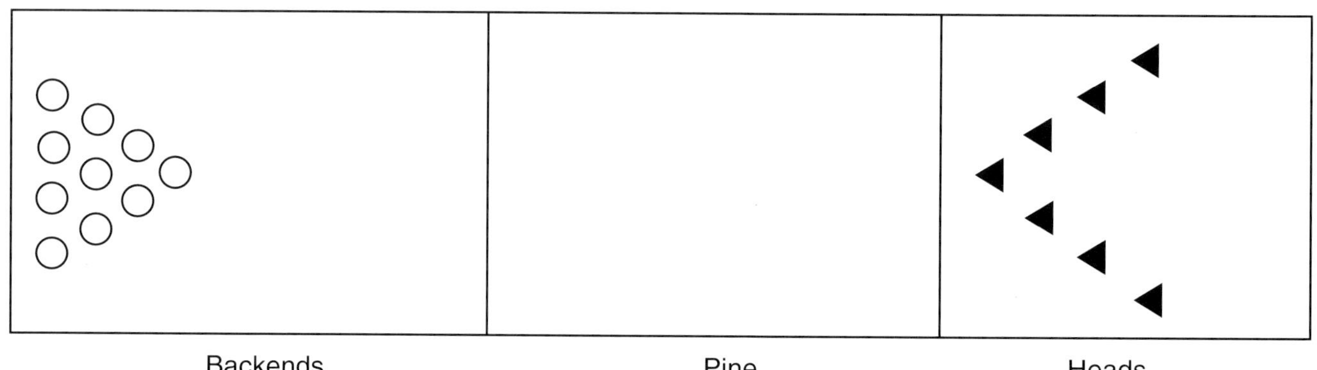

***Heads*** - Traditionally said to be the maple portion of the lane from the foul line (past the arrows) till it meets the pine area. However, on synthetic lanes this is more difficult to discern. Therefore, for ease of explanation we will consider the heads the first 20 feet of the lane.

***Pine*** - The pine starts roughly at the 20 foot point to approximately the 40 foot mark. Although the pine on a wood lane actually goes all the way to the pin deck, we will consider this middle 20 feet of the lane the Pine in terms of understanding ball reaction.

***Backends*** - As we have broken down the lane into 20 foot sections, this would represent the final 20 feet from the pine to the pins.

Each of the previously mentioned categories of static weights plays a certain roll in terms of ball reaction when compared to these three sections of the lane.

However, once again we must understand that the coverstock of the ball, the surface, and the ball construction all play a greater roll in determining ball reaction. Once that is understood, we can better understand how these weights relate to ball reaction.

***Heads*** - The static weights which come into play the most in the heads are Top or Bottom Weight, or Zero Balance. As a general rule, the greater the amount of Top Weight, the longer the ball will skid through the heads area on the lane.

Conversely, if the ball is balanced with Bottom Weight, it will begin to pick up an earlier roll through the heads. Finally, if the ball has neither Top nor Bottom Weight, but is said to have a Zero Balance, it will produce minimum skid through the heads and provide a reaction of even roll.

***Pine*** - The weights most relevant in this area of the lane are either Finger Weight, Thumb Weight, or Zero Balance. Once again, these weights are designed to influence ball reaction as the ball rolls through the middle portion of the lane.

In the pines, Finger Weight will help the ball to skid through this area of the lane, while Thumb Weight will initiate an earlier roll. Zero Balance will produce a minimal amount of skid, with a fairly even rolling pattern.

***Backends*** - The only set of weights not yet used are Right Side, Left Side and Zero Balance. These become the most influential weights as the ball rolls through the last 1/3 of the lane.

On the backends, Right Side Weight will help the ball to create more of a hooking action, producing the strongest backend reaction of these three. Just the opposite, Left Side Weight (for a right-handed bowler) will produce the least amount of hook in this area of the lane. Zero Balance will create a medium reaction, which commonly results in an arcing motion opposed to a strong hook.

# MATCHING STATIC WEIGHTS TO LANE CONDITIONS

Based on these reactions, lets study three different lane conditions for our three different categories of bowlers (assuming all are using three piece equipment).

For the purpose of identifying lane conditions, the following distances will be assumed (figure 5.9).

**5.9 - Dry Lane Condition:**

**5.9 - Medium Lane Condition:**

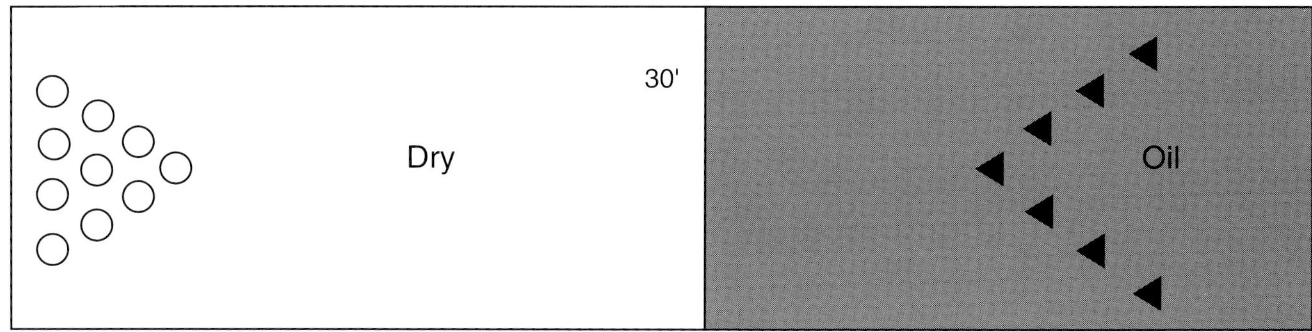


**5.9 - Oily Lane Condition:**

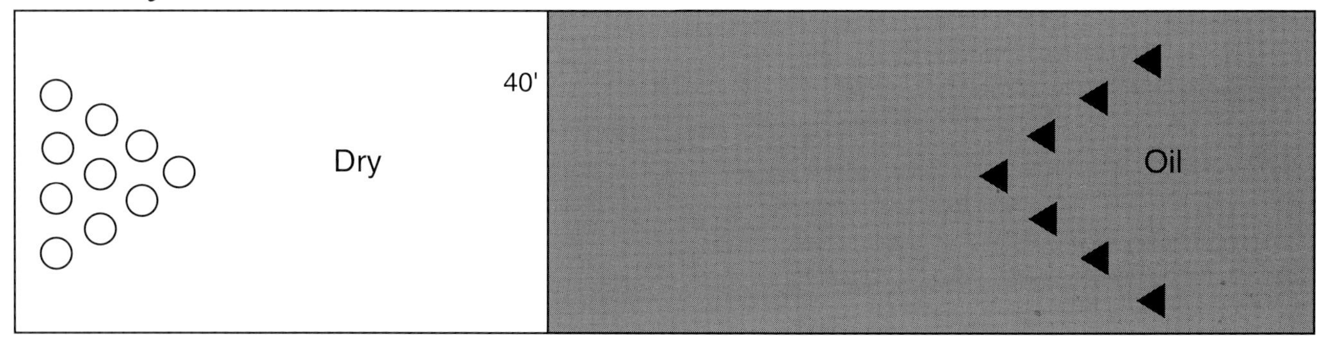


* Dry Lanes are said to be oiled to 18 - 25 feet or less
* Medium lanes are said to be oiled 25 - 35 feet
* Oily lanes are said to be oiled 35 - 45 feet or more

## STRAIGHT PLAYER

As we will see, each player will have their own combination of weights for these conditions. Keep in mind that for the Straight Player, the ball reaction is based on a bowler with average to above average ball speed, and minimal hook (5 boards or less from the breakpoint) (figure 5.10 next page).

 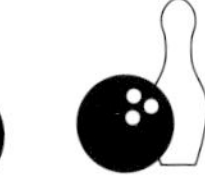

**5.10 - Straight Player**

***Dry Lanes*** = Zero Balance or Top Weight, Zero Balance or Finger Weight, Right Side Weight

This combination will keep the ball from rolling too early, but will still allow the ball to roll, and could produce the largest hook the Straight Player will experience.

***Medium Lanes*** = Bottom Weight or Zero Balance, Thumb Weight or Zero Balance, Right Side Weight

As the lanes have more oil in this example, the Straight Player will need the ball to pick up an earlier roll to assure adequate reaction on the backends. This combination should provide this reaction.

***Oily Lanes*** = Bottom Weight, Thumb Weight, Right Side Weight

On this condition, the Straight Player needs the earliest possible roll to produce a slight reaction on the backends. This combination, when combined with the appropriate coverstock (reactive) and surface (washed) should produce the earliest reaction possible (given the three piece construction).

## STROKER PLAYER

The Stroker Player is considered to have medium speed, medium release action, and a hook covering between 5 - 10 boards from the breakpoint on a medium lane condition (figure 5.11).

**5.11 - Stroker Player**

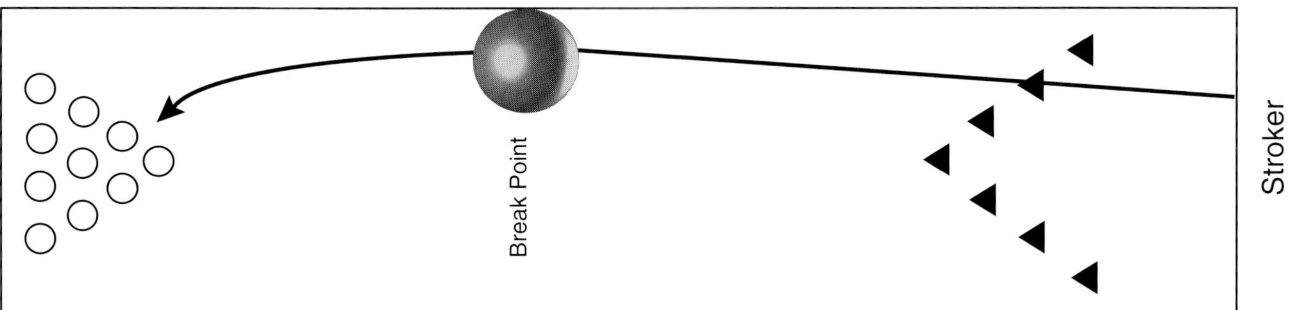

***Dry Lanes*** = Top Weight, Finger Weight, and Zero Balance or Right Side Weight

As the Stroker Player does have a medium hook, this player needs this combination to allow the ball to skid to the breakpoint without hooking too early. Zero Balance could be used to control backend reaction, if the lanes are breaking sharply.

***Medium Lanes*** = Top Weight or Zero Balance, Thumb Weight or Zero Balance, Right Side Weight

This combination of weights will allow the Stroker to initiate medium to early roll, depending on the needs produced from the lane condition. Also, the Right Side Weight should help the ball to sustain a strong finish on the backends.

***Oily Lanes*** = Zero Balance to Bottom Weight, Thumb Weight, Right Side Weight

Similar to the Straight Player, the Stroker needs the ball to begin rolling early to allow it to react on the backends. If the ball initially skids too far on this condition, it will not react on the backends. This combination should help to produce this reaction.

## HOOK BALL PLAYER

The Hook Ball Player is considered a player with average to above average ball speed, combined with a strong release, producing a hook of 10 or more boards from the breakpoint (figure 5.12).

**5.12 - Hook Ball Player**

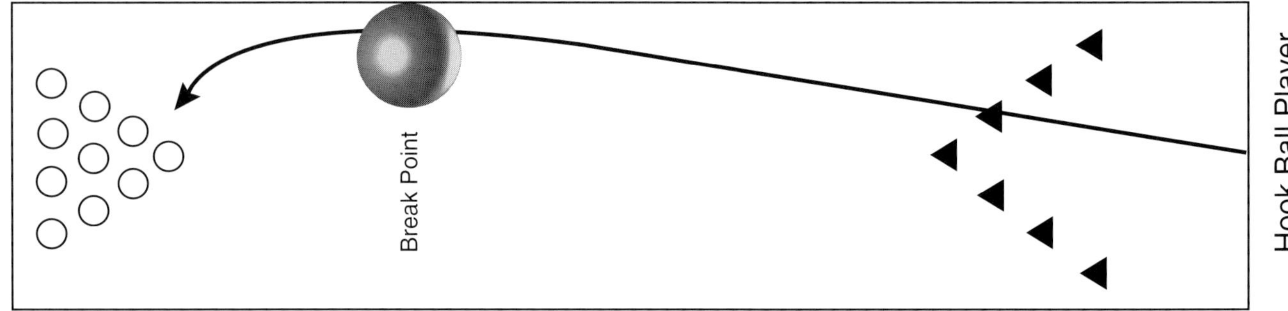


***Dry lanes*** = Top Weight, Finger Weight, Left Side Weight or Zero Balance

As the Hook Ball Player creates maximum revolutions and rotation through his release, he needs a ball which will be controllable when the lanes are dry. The above combination, along with a highly polished surface and a three piece, non reactive ball would be the best choice for this condition.

***Medium Lanes*** = Top Weight, Finger Weight, Right Side Weight

On this condition, the Hook Ball Players can really "open up" the lanes by creating a large area in which they can hit to reach the pocket. This is the benefit their style creates. The above combination of weights will allow the ball to skid to the breakpoint, then maximize the backend reaction for usually devastating results!

***Oily Lanes*** = Zero Balance or Top Weight, Zero Balance or Finger Weight, Zero Balance or Right Side Weight

The combination really depends on the overall lane condition in this case. If the lanes are very heavily oiled, the Zero Balances are the choice as it will allow the ball to roll fairly early, but still reach the breakpoint. Also, Zero Balance for backend reaction is usually a good choice as the ball will remain controllable and not give the bowler an "over - under" reaction.

The weights recommended above should be used as a guideline. Other combinations may be used depending on the exact condition on which the bowler is competing. However, these do represent a starting point when combined with the coverstock, surface, and core design to playing these conditions at a high level.

## CONCLUSIONS

The most important element which can be learned from this chapter is that Static Weights primarily influence the ball reaction of three piece bowling balls. However, comprehending these weights will only help us to understand the core positions explained in the next chapter.

Additionally, the following chapter covering Dynamics will show that ball balance will produce more influence on the balls reaction than the static weights. However, factors such as the bowlers style, the balls coverstock, surface, construction, and the lane condition must all be taken into account when analyzing the overall reaction of a ball.

As bowlers, we must always remember that no matter how technical and advanced we make our bowling equipment, the ball will not make up for a deficient physical game. The ability to repeat shots and hit a target on a consistent basis are always going to be the fundamentals of our sport. It is only after these criteria have been achieved that advanced equipment will help to improve our scores.

**5.13 - Static Balance Review**

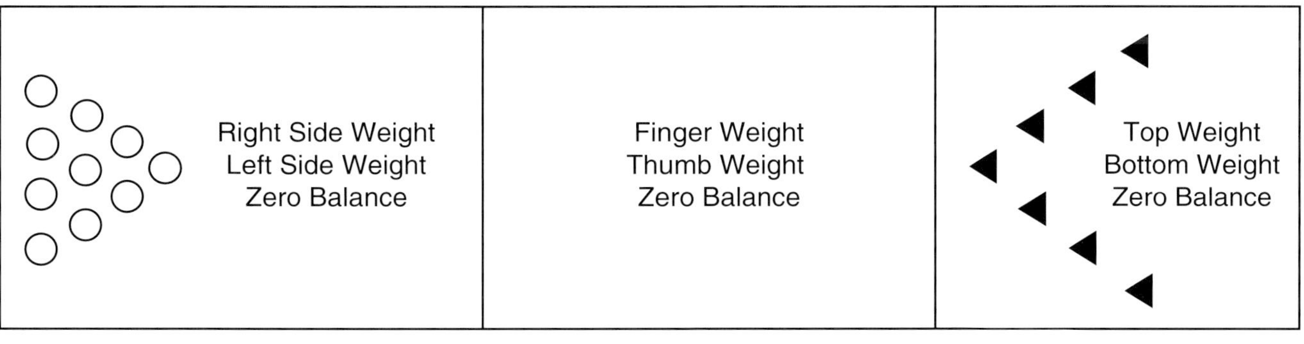

| | Straight Player | Stroker | Hook Ball Player |
|---|---|---|---|
| **Dry Lanes** | Top Weight/ Zero Balance<br>Finger Weight/ Zero Balance<br>Right Side Weight | Top Weight<br>Finger Weight<br>Right Side Weight/ Zero Balance | Top Weight<br>Finger Weight<br>Left Side Weight/ Zero Balance |
| **Medium Lanes** | Bottom Weight/ Zero Balance<br>Thumb Weight/ Zero Balance<br>Right Side Weight | Top Weight/ Zero Balance<br>Thumb Weight/ Zero Balance<br>Right Side Weight | Top Weight<br>Finger Weight<br>Right Side Weight |
| **Oily Lanes** | Bottom Weight<br>Thumb Weight<br>Right Side Weight | Bottom Weight/ Zero Balance<br>Thumb Weight<br>Right Side Weight | Top Weight/ Zero Balance<br>Finger Weight/ Zero Balance<br>Right Side Weight/ Zero Balance |

So, now that we are equipped with the knowledge of Static Weights, lets explore why Dynamic Balance plays a more important role in determining ball reaction.

# Chapter 6

The message throughout chapter 5 was that static weights truly relate best to three piece designed bowing balls. In addition, it was noted that dynamic balance is what measures the reaction of two piece designed balls.

Therefore, to borrow a statement from the previous chapter;

***Static Weights are Not nearly as important as the position and Dynamic Balance of the weight block in the bowling ball.***

The basis for this statement comes from the differences in densities, position of the weight block, and overall mass of the core.

To help in understanding this concept, lets look at the following example;

Ball A has been placed in an upright position, with the line representing equal halves of the bowling ball (figure 6.1). In this example, it would be easy to reason that the ball would be evenly balanced (right side vs left side) if weighed on a static beam balance (Do Do Scale).

Ball B has been placed in an unbalanced position (which will be discussed shortly) with the line in this example clearly showing that more of the weight has been placed on the right side of the ball (figure 6.2). However, with the use of a balance hole, as shown in the example, the ball can be evenly balanced when weighed in the Do Do scale (comparing the right side vs the left side) just as Ball A. However, will they react the same when they are rolled down the lane? As this chapter will show, their reactions will be very different.

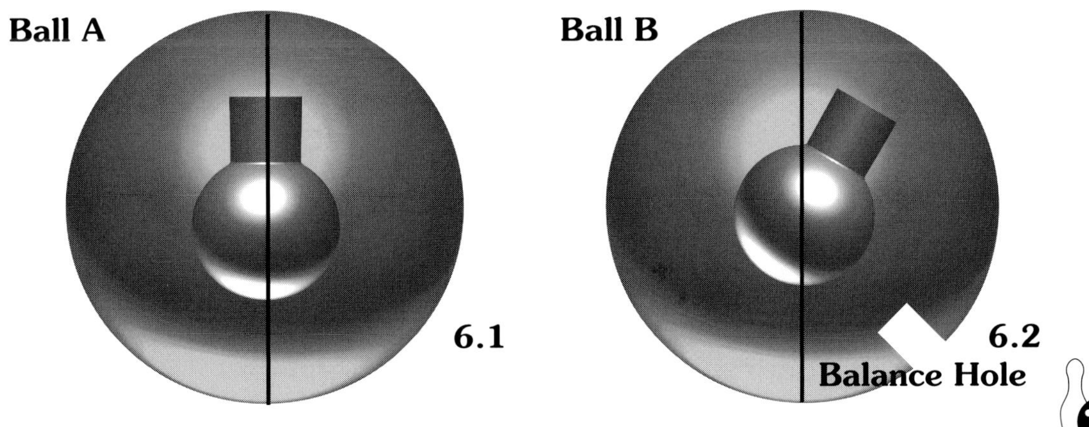


6.1

6.2

The vast majority of today's bowling balls are constructed with a two piece design or a design similar to this but with more pieces. Therefore, it should be easy to understand that balancing a ball by this method is truly more effective with today's equipment.

## UNDERSTANDING THE "PIN"

In Chapter 4 we discussed ball construction based on three core designs. They were;

Three Piece
Two Piece Center Heavy
Two Piece Cover Heavy

When discussing the pin, it is important to understand that only two of these designs use a pin which will be relevant to determining ball reaction. They are both "Two Piece" designs. During manufacturing, a pin is used to hold the weight block in place, as the coverstock is poured around the weight block in its mold, as shown in figure 6.3.

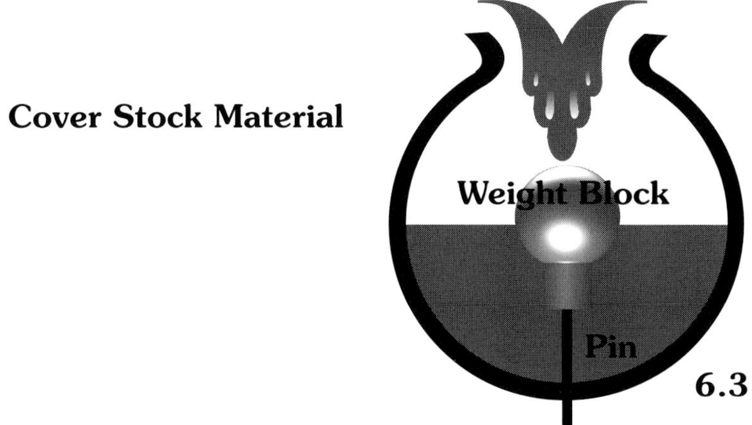

6.3

Therefore, this pin represents the top of the weight block. Hence, when balancing the weight block in different positions for various reactions, the pin is used to attain the desired core position/balance.

Another important element to understand concerning the pin, is its relation to the Center of Gravity (CG). When the pin is located within 1 1/2 inches of the CG, the pin is considered in a "Pin - In" position. Conversely, when the pin is located further than 1 1/2 inches from the CG, the pin is considered in a Pin - Out position. Figures 6.4 and 6.5 show both of these positions.

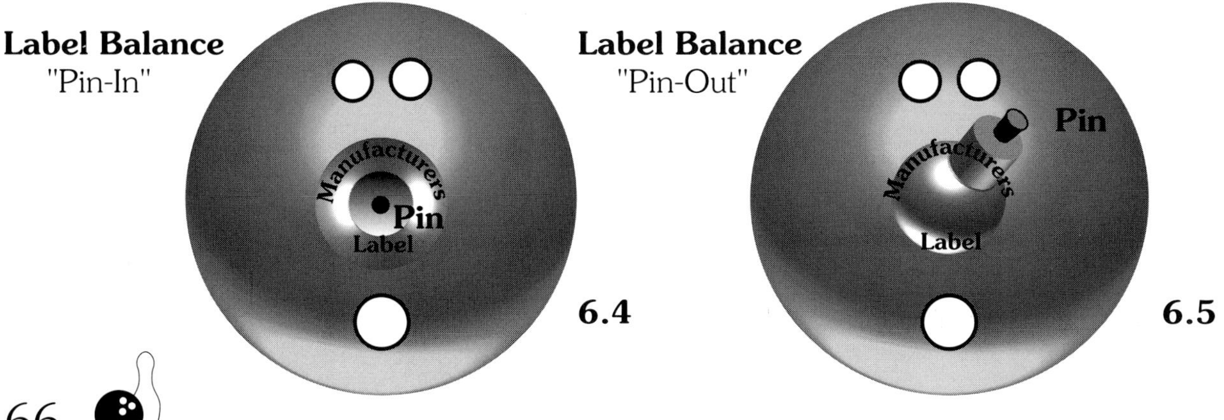

6.4

6.5

The position of the pin to the CG, for our understanding, simply tells us how the weight block is situated in the ball with relation to the center of gravity. As always, the pin is still the determining factor in the overall reaction of the ball as it rolls down the lane. The position of the Center of Gravity simply compliments the reaction of the weight block balance.

To better understand the Pin - In and Pin - Out positions, as well as how the core designs are effected by dynamic balance, we need to understand how the weight block can be balanced from the standpoint of Stability.

## WEIGHT BLOCK STABILITY

One of the major factors in understanding dynamic balance is to understand how weight blocks can be balanced based on their stability. There are three examples we will use to show how a core design can be balanced from either a stable or unstable position.

For this example we will use a standard two piece designed core.

#1 - In figure 6.6 we notice that the weight block is in a perpendicular position in relation to the axis line. Its stability in this position would be similar to a bowling pin in an upright position.

In the same way, the weight block will remain "stable" if drilled in this position in a bowling ball. Recalling the explanation of the "axis line" (chapter 4) the weight block would be positioned in a perpendicular fashion (90 degrees) to the axis line. Therefore, as the ball rolls down the lane, the weight block will rotate in an "end over end" manner. As we will see later in the chapter, this position will produce initial skid with medium to minimal hook as the ball rolls down the lane.

#2 - In figure 6.7, we notice that the weight block is lying in a horizontal position. In this case, the stability of the weight block would be compared to a bowling pin lying in the same fashion.

Figure 6.7 shows, the weight block would be evenly positioned around the axis line. Here, the ball would have a greater tendency to roll, as all of its mass is positioned on the axis line, but would still be considered in a stable position. This core position would initiate an early roll with an even reaction as the ball rolls down the lane. Backend reaction would be an "arcing" motion with medium to minimum hook.

#3 - In this final example, figure 6.8 shows the weight block is in a position which is considered unstable. Contrary to the first two examples, the weight block in this position is similar to a bowling pin when it is leaning on its edge. The pin will most likely fall to the deck or stand up, in either case reaching a stable position.

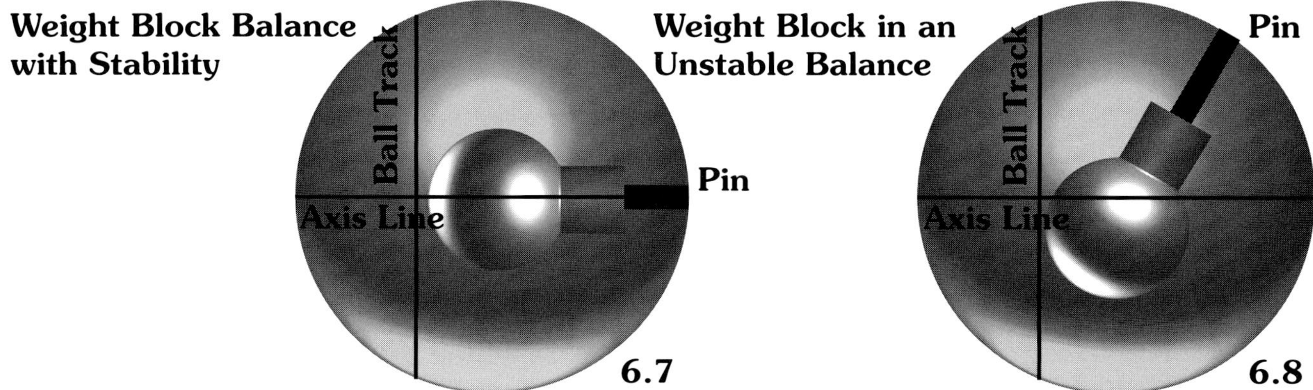


When a core design is positioned in this unstable manner, the top of the weight block is at a 45 degree angle to the axis line. However, as the ball rolls down the lane, the weight block will progress to a stable position of an end over end roll. Ultimately, the weight block will reach the same position as shown in example #1. This progression will cause a track flare which is shown in figure 6.9.

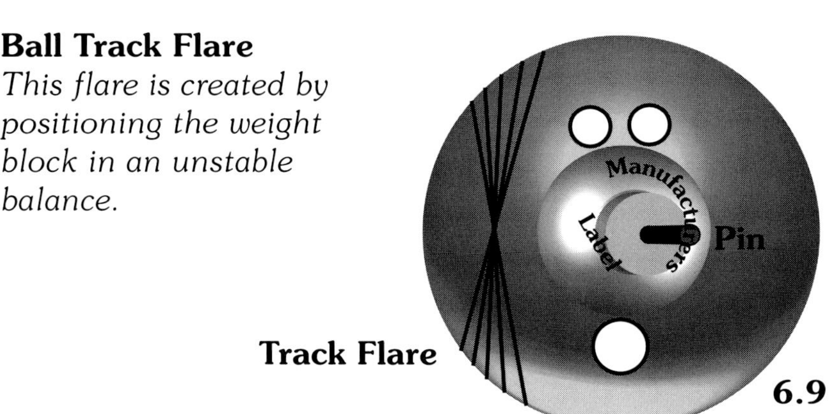


**Ball Track Flare**
*This flare is created by positioning the weight block in an unstable balance.*

This flare is very beneficial in terms of ball reaction. The effects of track flare will be covered later in this chapter. However, in terms of ball reaction, this unstable position will create initial skid, with very strong backend reaction.

Each of the previous examples directly relates to a specific balance used to achieve various ball reactions. The following section will explain each of these in greater detail, as well as other balances used to attain a variety of ball reactions.

## HOW THE PIN POSITION RELATES TO STATIC BALANCE

Before detailing ball reaction based on dynamic balance, we first need to understand how the position of the pin makes the ball react in similar ways to static weights.

 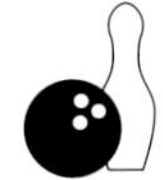

Recalling chapter 5 and the explanation of static weights, the following reactions were understood;

Finger Weight = Longer skid through the middle portion of the lane (Pines)
Thumb Weight = Earlier roll through the middle portion of the lane
Zero Balance = Minimal initial skid with an even roll

These held true for both right and left-handed players, and controlled a three piece ball as it rolled through the middle portion of the lane. With the two piece design, the pin can be substituted for these weights to achieve the same reaction characteristics.

This is achieved in the following manner;

To achieve a reaction of **longer skid**, with delayed back end reaction (similar to Finger Weight) the pin is placed in a position above the mid line. The mid line being the line which runs through the center of the bowlers grip and around the exterior of the ball (figure 6.10).

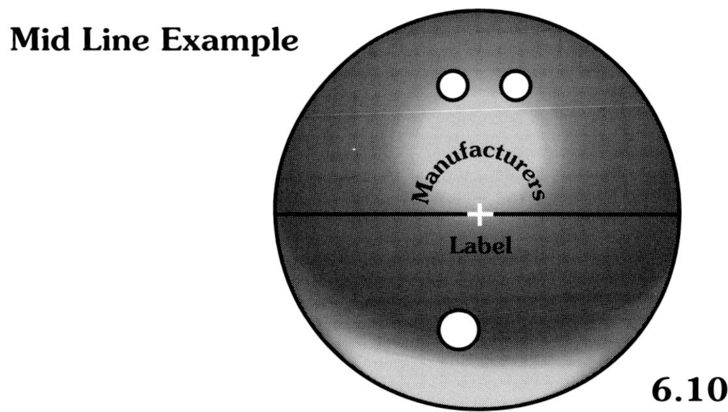

6.10

The further the pin is placed above the mid line, the more the ball reacts like Finger Weight and will produce more skid.

If an **earlier roll** is desired (similar to Thumb Weight), the pin is positioned below the mid line. Once again, the lower the pin is placed below the mid line, the earlier the ball will begin to roll.

An **even roll** is therefore achieved by placing the pin on the mid line. This will produce a reaction similar to Zero Balance, and will provide a more even and predictable roll.

## DYNAMICALLY BALANCING A BOWLING BALL FOR SPECIFIC REACTIONS

The three balances explained in the previous section relate to the four most common balances drilled into bowling balls. These are;

Label Balance
Leverage Balance
Axis Balance
Leverage Axis Balance

These balances represent four distinct reactions for a bowling ball as it rolls down the lane, and will be covered at length later in this chapter. However, it is important to understand how these balances are determined. This is accomplished by understanding dynamic quadrants.

## DYNAMIC QUADRANTS

The two common factors which all bowlers share are the ball track and axis point (figure 6.11). The location of these are greatly determined by the bowlers physical game and release. However, these represent the starting points when determining how to balance a ball for a specific bowler.

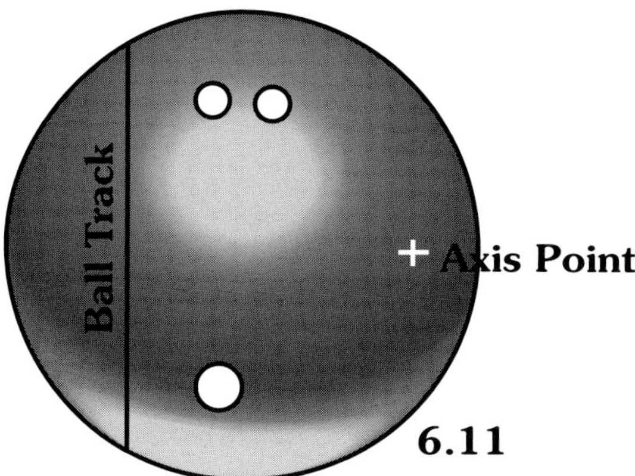

6.11

Each of the previously mentioned balances represents a certain distance from the bowlers axis. Figure 6.12 shows a range of dynamic quadrants which are used when determining ball reaction. Dynamic Quadrants are used the same for right and left-handed bowlers.

**Dynamic Quadrants**

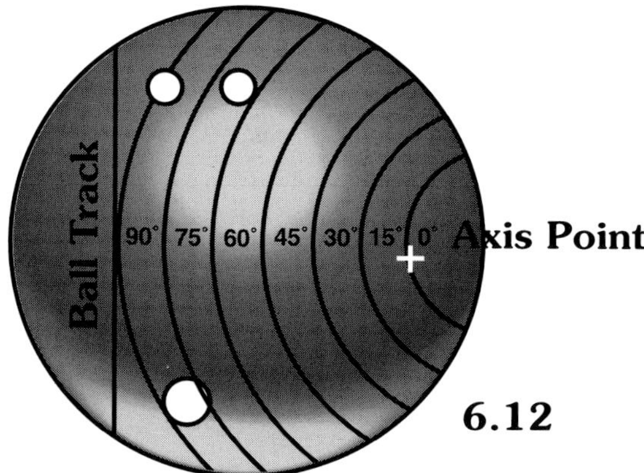

6.12

The key to understanding dynamic quadrants is as follows;

*Every 1 1/8th of an inch from the bowlers axis to the bowlers ball track represents 15 degrees. For example, 3 3/8ths of an inch from the axis point, towards the center of the grip, represents 45 degrees, more commonly known as Leverage Balance (figure 6.13).

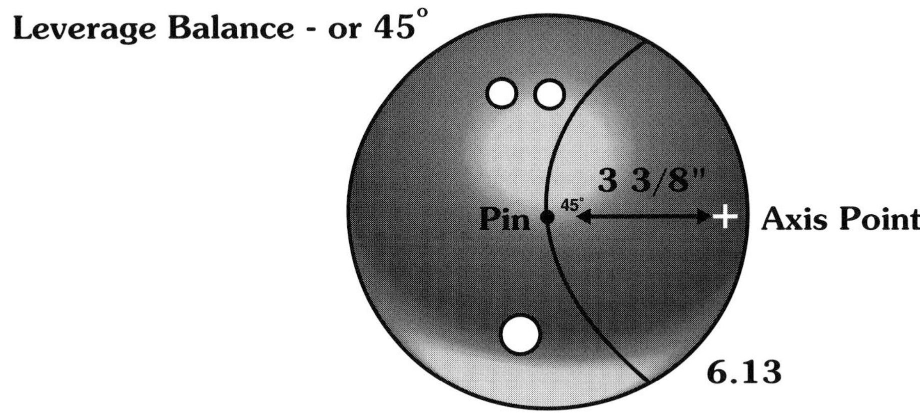

6.13

To help in understanding this concept, lets look at the following example.

Bowler A is a high track player, and has an axis point of 5 1/2 inches from the center of grip. Conversely, Bowler B has a much lower ball track, further from the finger and thumb holes, translating to an axis point of 3 1/2 inches from the center of grip (figure 6.14).

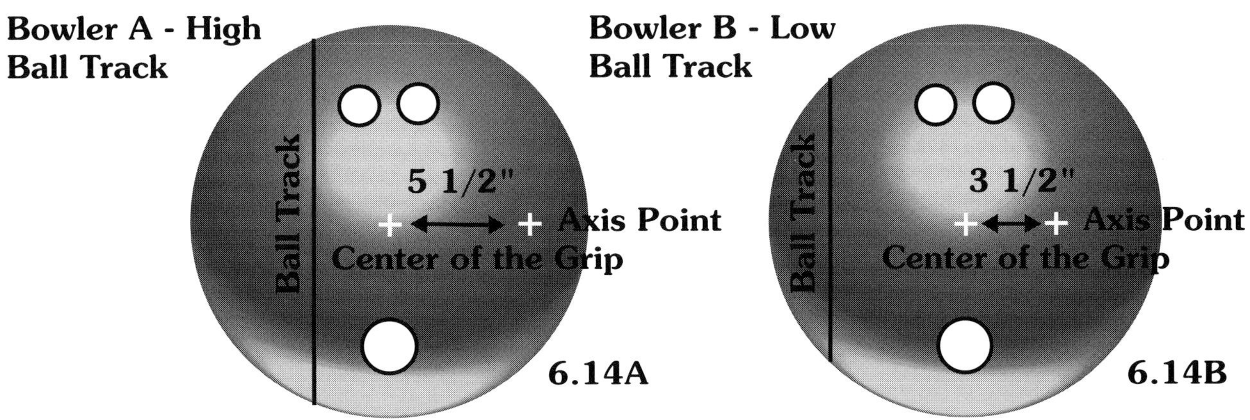

6.14A

6.14B

Based on the concept of 1 1/8 of an inch equalling 15 degrees, the following would hold true for each of these bowlers:

| | Bowler A | Bowler B |
|---|---|---|
| Zero Degrees | 5 1/2 | 3 1/2 |
| 15 degrees | 4 3/8 | 2 3/8 |
| 30 degrees | 3 1/4 | 1 1/4 |
| 45 degrees | 2 1/8 | 1/8 |
| 60 degrees | 1 | - 1 |
| 75 degrees | - 1/8 | - 2 1/8 |
| 90 degrees | - 1 1/4 | - 3 1/4 |

*Negative numbers indicate the pin is being positioned left of the bowlers grip.

Figure 6.15 shows that both bowlers would have a unique set of quadrants based on their ball track and axis point.

**Bowler A - Dynamic Quadrants**

Ball Track

90° 75° 60° 45° 30° 15° 0° Axis Point

6.15A

**Bowler B - Dynamic Quadrants**

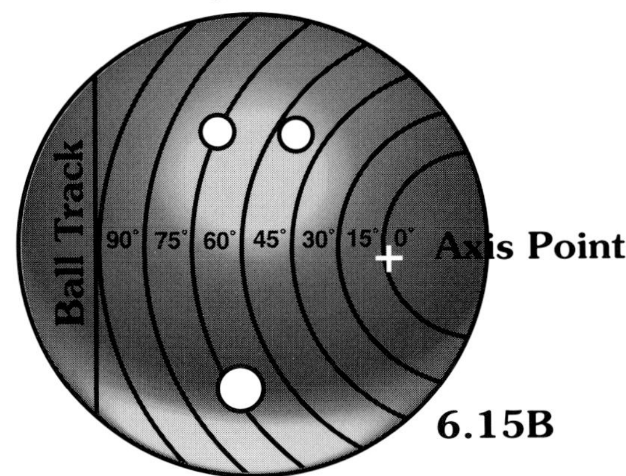


6.15B

Additionally, 45 degrees or Leverage Balance would be in a different position for each player. Bowler A would have the pin 2 1/8 inches from the grip for Leverage Balance, while Bowler B would only have the pin positioned 1/8th of an inch from the center of the grip for the same balance.

Therefore, in the following example, Bowler A would have the pin positioned in the "traditional" rage of 2" from the center of grip for Leverage Balance, while Bowler B will have the pin positioned 1/8 of an inch from the center of the grip for the same balance (figure 6.16).

**Bowler A - Leverage Balance**

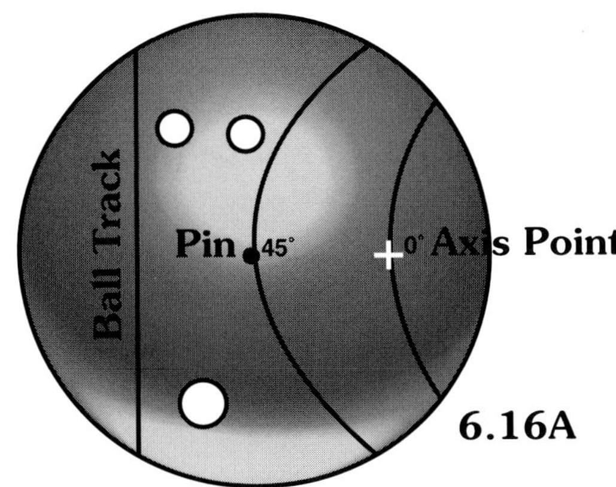


6.16A

**Bowler B - Leverage Balance**

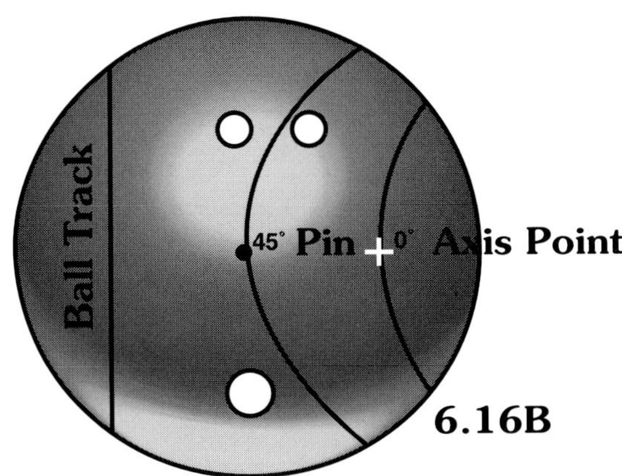


6.16B

When looking at the pin position for Bowler B, it appears to be in the "traditional" area for Label Balance. However, based on the knowledge of Dynamic Quadrants, it is easy to understand that this position would actually represent a leverage position based on the track and axis points.

The golden rule is to use dynamic quadrants when determining a desired reaction. Therefore, as you proceed through this chapter, recall your axis point (chapter 4) as it will assist you in understanding how your game relates to the balances discussed. This will allow you to comprehend ball reaction with each of these balances, while keeping in perspective the position in which the pin will be placed based on your specific ball track and axis point.

# LABEL BALANCE

Without question, Label Balance is the most common balance used when drilling bowling balls. The reason being, it suites the biggest majority of bowlers. Also, it is a balance that is predictable. In fact, a number of World Champion bowlers use only this balance and change the coverstock, surface characteristics, and ball construction for the various lane conditions.

As the name implies, Label Balance simply consists of drilling the ball with the grip being positioned somewhere over the label. The ball reaction is therefore determined by the position of the pin (figure 6.17).

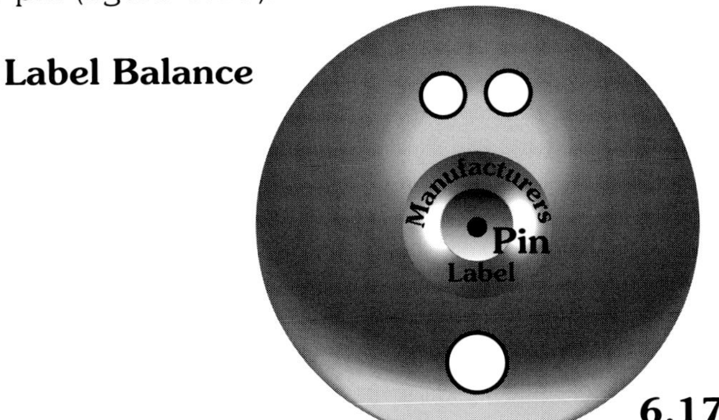


6.17

A true "end over end" roll is only achieved when the pin is positioned in the ball track. In this manner, the track is at a 90 degree angle from the axis line. This will provide the longest skid with the least amount of back end reaction. Therefore, the further the pin is located from the ball track, the more the weight block becomes unbalanced (unstable), and provides a stronger backend reaction.

Therefore, one important element to remember in Label Balance is that in this position, the weight block is still in a slightly unbalanced position. Additionally, the further the pin is "out" the more the ball will react in an unstable fashion, and will provide a stronger back end reaction.

# HOW TO ACHIEVE A VARIETY OF BALL REACTIONS USING LABEL BALANCE

## LABEL BALANCE - LONGER SKID

A ball having the pin positioned "in" and above the mid line will produce initial skid with minimal to medium back end reaction.

Whereas, a ball having the pin positioned "out" and above the mid line (figure 6.18) will produce greater initial skid with medium to maximum backend reaction.

## LABEL BALANCE - EARLIER ROLL

A Pin - In ball with the pin positioned below the mid line will produce an earlier roll, with minimal to medium backend reaction.

Whereas, a Pin - Out ball with the pin positioned below the mid line (figure 6.19) will produce an earlier roll with medium to maximum back end reaction.

** When using these pin down drillings, the ball track will be higher than normal, due to the pin position. Therefore, these drillings are not usually recommended for players who track close to the thumb hole, as the ball track may roll over the thumb hole.*

** Additionally, as these drillings initiate an earlier ball roll, less of the balls "energy" will be saved for the backends. Therefore, the backend reaction will be reduced when compared to the other examples using Label Balance.*

## LABEL BALANCE - EVEN ROLL

A Pin - In ball drilled on the mid line will produce a reaction of minimal initial skid with minimal to medium backend reaction.

Whereas, a Pin - Out ball drilled on the mid line (figure 6.20) will produce a reaction of medium initial skid with medium to maximum back end reaction.

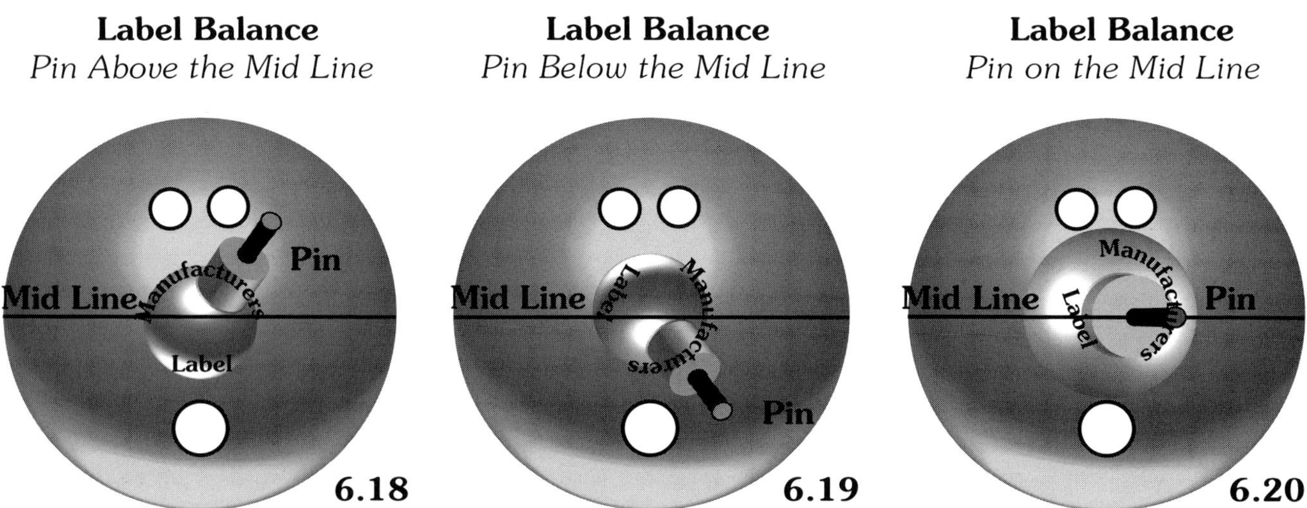


Once again, it is important to remember that the position of the pin for Label Balance is determined by your ball track and axis point. As shown in the Dynamic Quadrants section, two bowlers with different axis points will have the pin positioned in different areas to achieve the same reaction.

For example, if a 60 degree position was desired, the pin could be placed in a range either left or right of the bowlers grip, depending on the players axis point (figure 6.21 - next page).

**60° Pin - High Track Bowler**

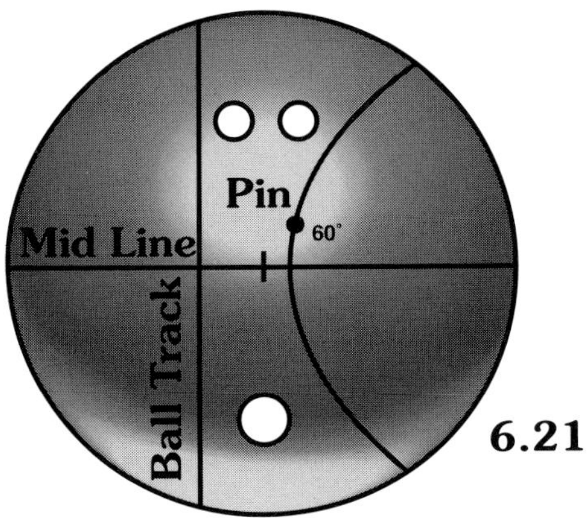


**60° Pin - Low Track Bowler**

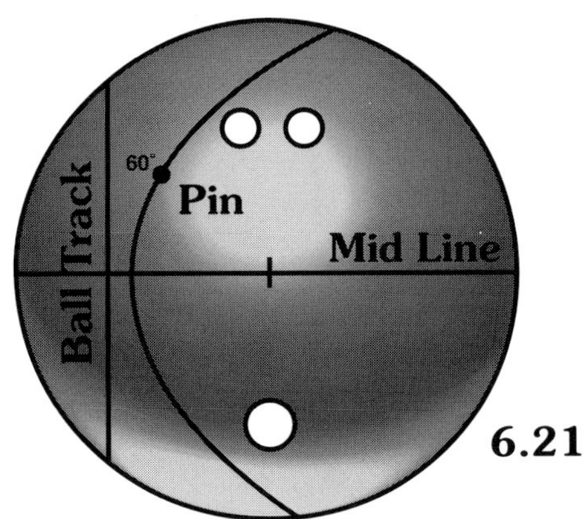


**6.22 - Label Balance Reaction - Right-Handed**

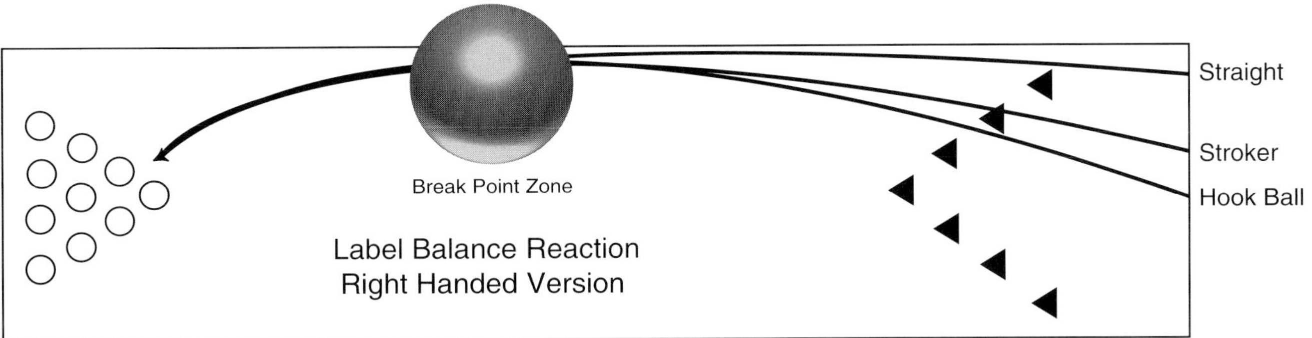


**6.22 - Label Balance Reaction - Left-Handed**

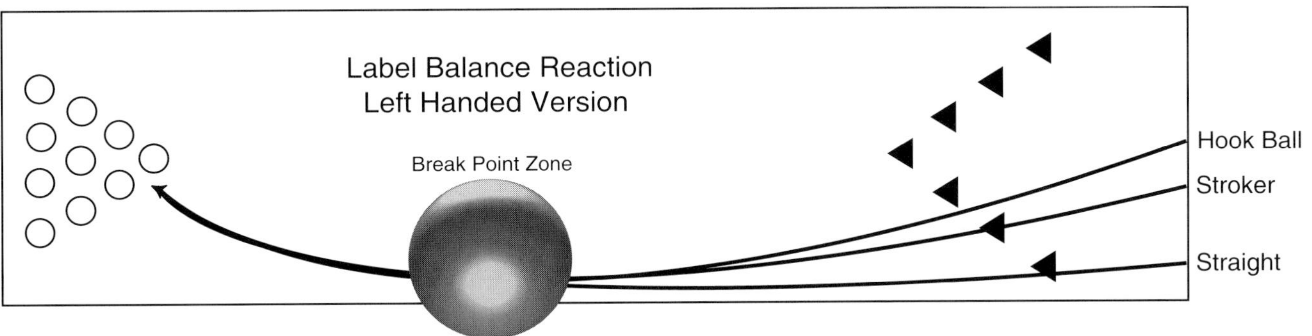


# LEVERAGE BALANCE

Given the fact that Label Balance is the most commonly drilled balance, Leverage Balance, or a form of it, is most likely the second most popular drilling. Once again, it is not uncommon to find players strictly using this balance in all of their bowling balls, while altering the coverstock, surface, and ball construction when adjusting to various conditions.

Leverage Balance differs from Label and Axis Balance in that the weight block in this case is positioned between both of these points. Although there are many forms of Leverage Balance, and various methods pro shops use for drilling it, we will consider Leverage Balance to be a 45 degree angle from the axis point. Therefore, as mentioned in the Dynamic Quadrants section, the most common method of finding your leverage position is to measure 3 3/8 inches in from the axis point, and place the pin on this location (figure 6.23)

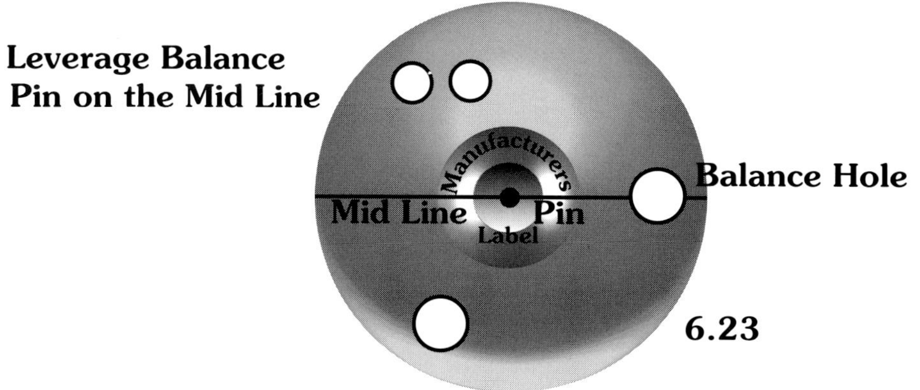

6.23

***Remember 1 1/8 represents 15 degrees on the bowling ball. Therefore 45 degrees would equal 1 1/8 x 3 or 3 3/8ths inches.***

As mentioned earlier, the ball track and axis line form a 90 degree angle. In addition, we stated that both of these positions were considered to be stable. Therefore, recalling the previous #3 example of Stability, Leverage Balance is at a position approximately half way between the ball track and axis point, thus in an unstable position (figure 6.24).

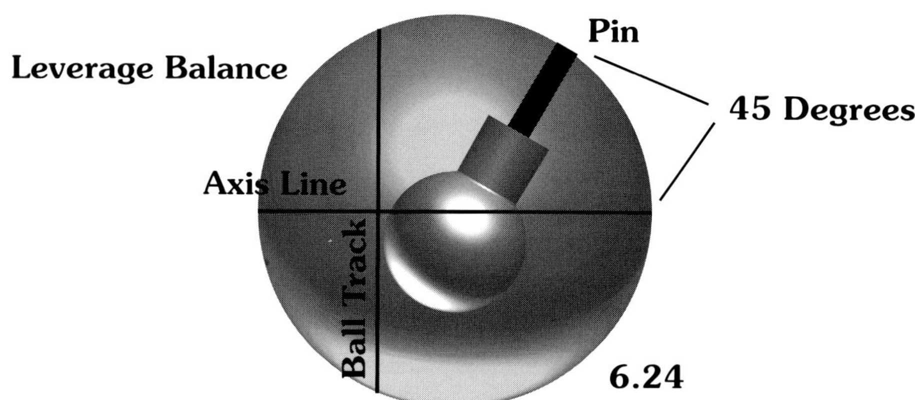

6.24

Being unstable, it was noted that the weight block will progress to a stable position as the ball rolls down the lane. This produces the increased back end reaction, and will cause the ball track to flare. This track flare is produced from the weight block making the ball alter its roll pattern as it progresses to the stable position.

## TRACK FLARE

Unfortunately, many bowlers perceive track flare to adversely affect ball reaction. Actually, this flare is a very beneficial tool once you understand its benefit. Each time the ball makes an

 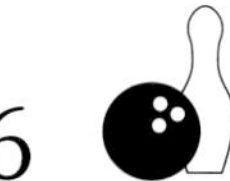

additional track, a fresh piece of the balls surface is coming in contact with the lane (figure 6.25).

**Track Flare**
This flare is created by positioning the weight block in an unstable balance.

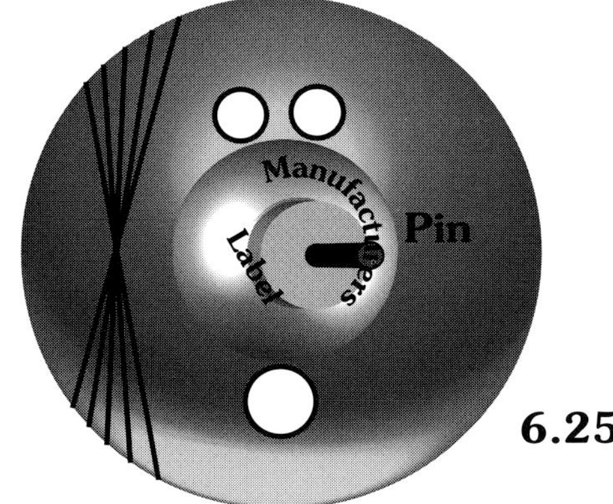


**6.25**

Conversely, when the weight block is in a stable position and rolls very even, the track has minimal flare. Therefore, there is always a certain amount of oil between the ball surface and the lane. This produces less traction on the backends, and therefore less reaction than when the track has a larger flare.

Generally, the track flares the most when the ball is on the last 1/2 of the lane. Usually this portion of the lane has less oil than the first 30 feet. Therefore, the fresh ball surface has a better chance to "grab" the lane surface.

In addition, certain core designs are more likely to create a large flare, even when balanced in a stable position. This is due to the Dynamics created by the weight block. The difference between a large flare and a narrow flare, is once again seen in the ball reaction, as it rolls down the lane.

The ball with a wider flare will have the tendency to roll earlier and react stronger on the backends, whereas a ball with a narrow flare will tend to skid slightly longer and react less violently and more evenly on the backends (figure 6.26).

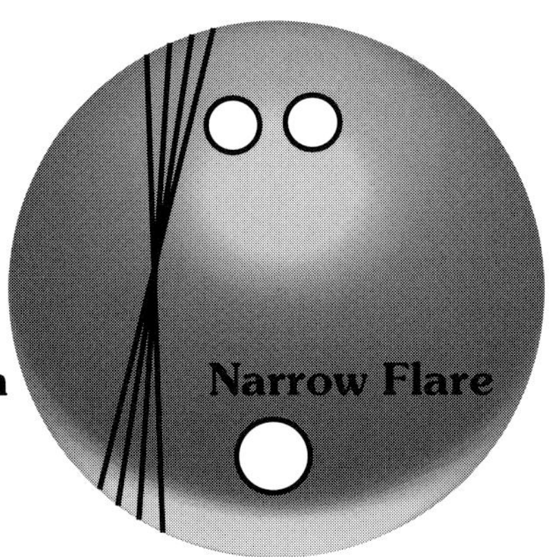


**6.26**
**Ball Track with Narrow Flare**

**6.26 - Narrow Flare Reaction**

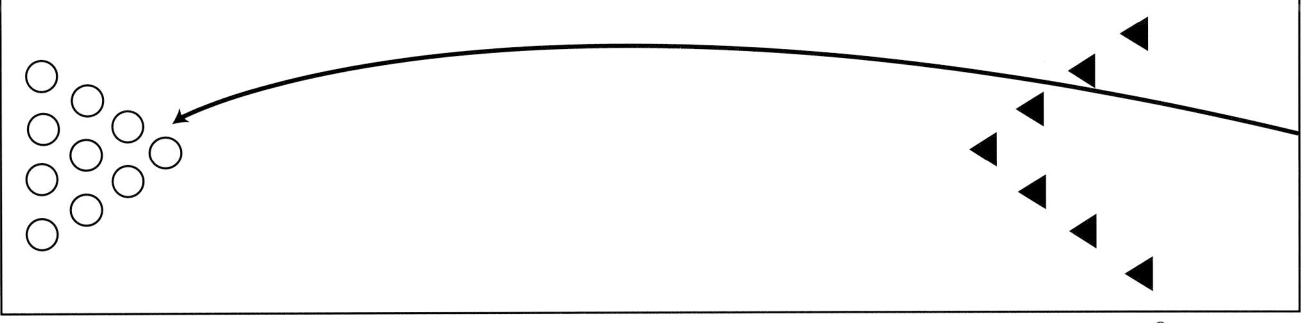

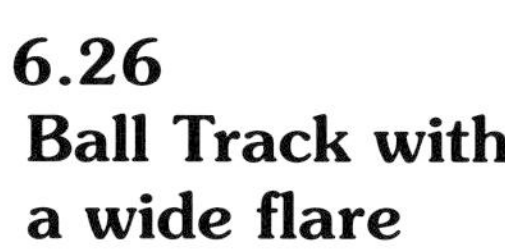

6.26
Ball Track with a wide flare

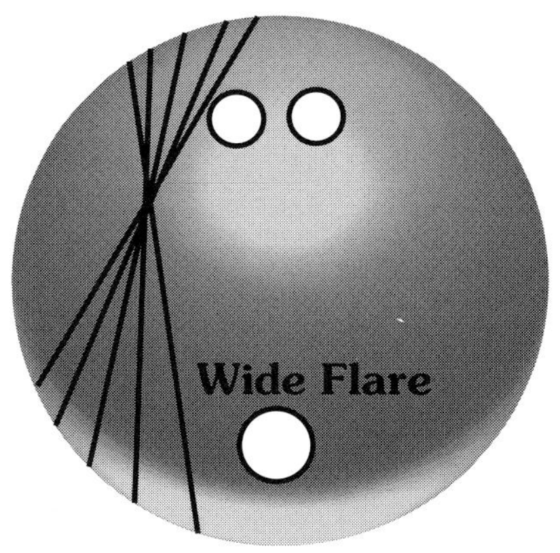


6.26 - Wide Flare Reaction

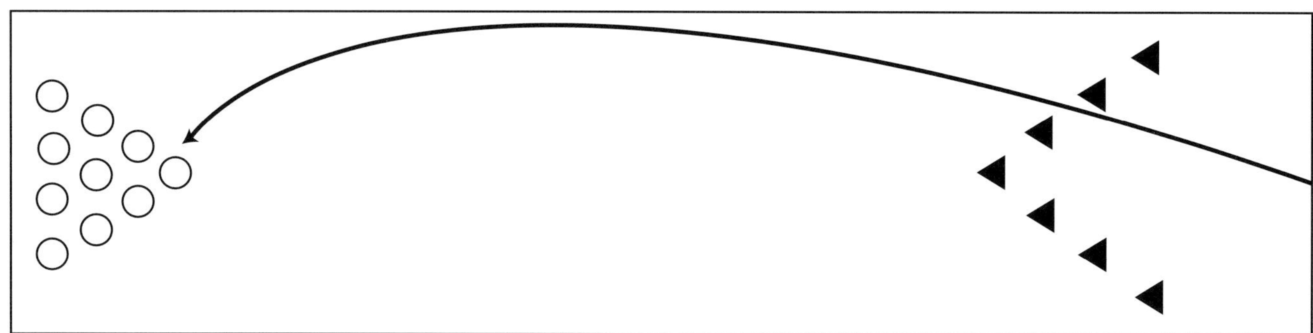

# WHO SHOULD USE LEVERAGE BALANCE?

Although any bowler can benefit from Leverage Balance (given the necessary coverstock , surface and ball construction) the type of player who gains the most benefit from this balance is the Stroker Player. This is especially true with today's reactive resin coverstocks.

For example, a Hook Ball Player bowling on a medium lane condition with a reactive resin ball, often finds the Leverage Balance uncontrollable. Lets consider the following factors.

1.) Leverage Balance provides maximum back end reaction.
2.) The lane is providing strong backends.
3.) The Hook Ball Players release creates a strong ball reaction on the back end of the lane.

Each one of these factors provides backend reaction. Therefore, when two or three of these elements are combined, there is a good chance that the ball will be very hard to control on a consistent basis. That is not to say that this balance will not work for the Hook Ball Player, given the proper surface and ball construction.

However, on a variety of lane conditions, the Stroker Player will generally gain more benefit from this balance.

# BALANCE HOLES

The final element of Leverage Balance deals with the position of the Balance Hole. This extra hole is used to balance the ball statically, and conform to the rule of 1 oz maximum side weight. However, a balance hole is not always necessary when drilling leverage weight. Lets look at the following examples.

***Ball #1***

A bowler selects a ball with the weight block in a "pin - out" position. The pin is determined to be "out" far enough to reach the bowlers leverage point, while keeping the center of gravity near the bowlers grip. Therefore, when weighed on the Do Do scale, the ball is found to still be "legal", although the pin is in a leverage position.

***Ball #2***

This bowler chooses a ball with the weight block in a "Pin - In" position, but wants the ball to be drilled with Leverage Balance. In this case, the pin is positioned at the leverage point, however when weighed on the Do Do scale the ball is found to weigh more than the allowable 1 oz of side weight. In this situation, a balance hole is required to reduce the amount of side weight and make the ball "legal".

In addition to balancing the ball statically, balance holes also have a significant influence on back end reaction. Factors such as the position, size and depth of the balance hole all have an effect on how the ball will react as it rolls down the lane.

## BALANCE HOLE POSITION

There are many positions in which balance holes can be drilled. The position, size and depth are usually determined by the pro shop operator based on the desired ball reaction. However, it is beneficial to understand their influence on the balls reaction. Therefore, we will study the two most common positions.

The most common position for a balance hole to be drilled is on the mid line. The exact position on the mid line is determined by the desired ball reaction. The following is the general rule in regards to the position;

***For an even roll - with less back end reaction the extra hole is drilled on the axis point (figure 6.27).***

***For longer skid - with a stronger back end reaction the extra hole is drilled below the axis point (figure 6.28).***

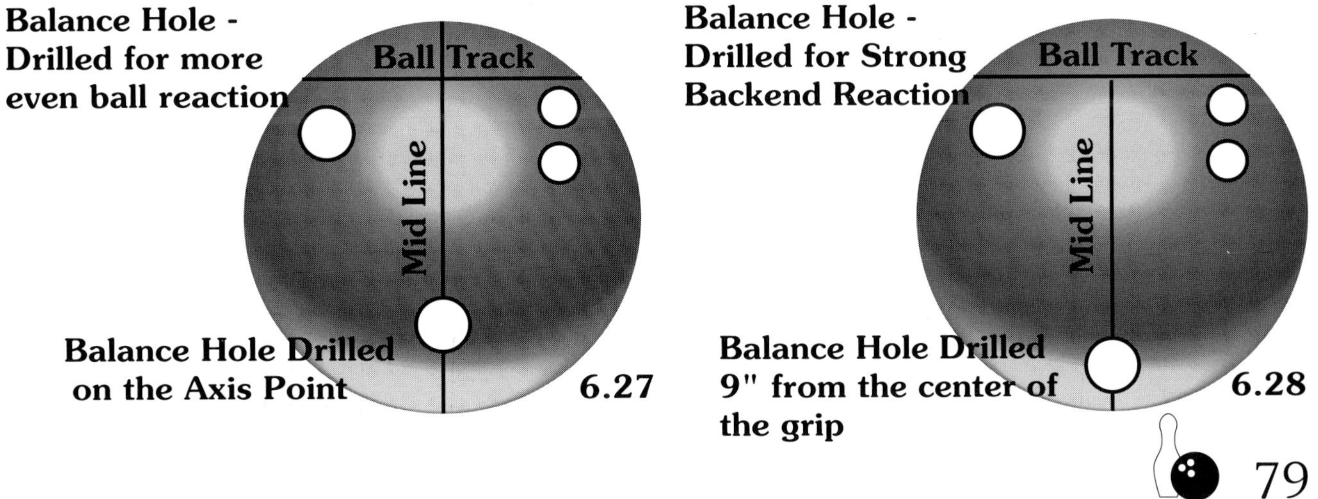

***Generally, the furthest position from the axis point, for the balance hole to be drilled, is 3 3/8ths of an inch below the axis point or 9 inches from the center of the grip.**

Therefore, a balance hole drilled 9 inches from the center of the grip (still on the mid line) will usually represent the maximum skid and strongest backend reaction. Conversely, a balance hole drilled on the axis point will produce a more even roll with reduced backend reaction.

### BALANCE HOLE SIZE AND DEPTH

The position of the balance hole represents the major influence concerning the balls reaction. However, the size and depth also contribute to ball reaction. The following rules generally apply;

***Stronger Backend Reaction = Drilling the Balance hole large and shallow***

***Even Roll with Moderate Backend Reaction = Drilling the Balance Hole small and Deep.***

These factors compliment the position of the balance hole in determining the balls overall reaction.

The message concerning balance holes is to work with your pro shop operator when determining the position, size and depth of the balance hole. They need to determine the flexibility of the ball (based on static limitations) in so far as determining the desired reaction, while maintaining the legal static balance.

## VARIOUS BALL REACTIONS BY USING LEVERAGE BALANCE

Just as a variety of ball reactions could be created by different pin placements with Label Balance, the same can be accomplished through the use of Leverage Balance.

### LEVERAGE BALANCE - LONGER SKID

1.) A Pin - Out ball is used and the pin is positioned above the leverage point (figure 6.29). This will provide a longer initial skid, with a strong backend reaction.

2.) A Pin - In ball is used with the Center of Gravity on or above the leverage point, and the pin once again placed above the leverage point and close to the finger holes. The balance hole is drilled on or below the axis point based on the desired back end reaction and static balance.

**Leverage Balance**
**Pin above the Mid Line**

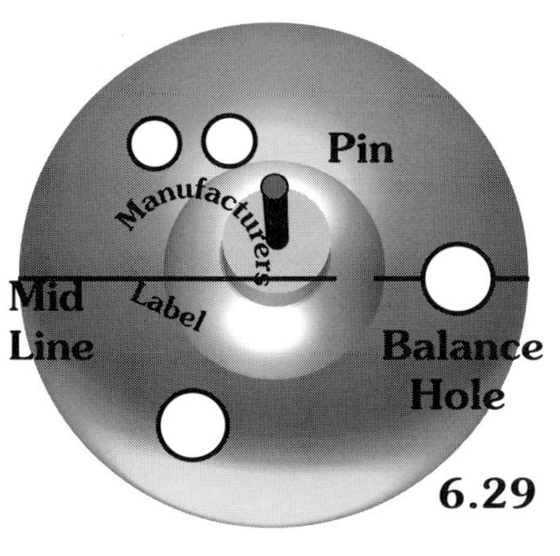


**Leverage Balance**
**Pin below the Mid Line**

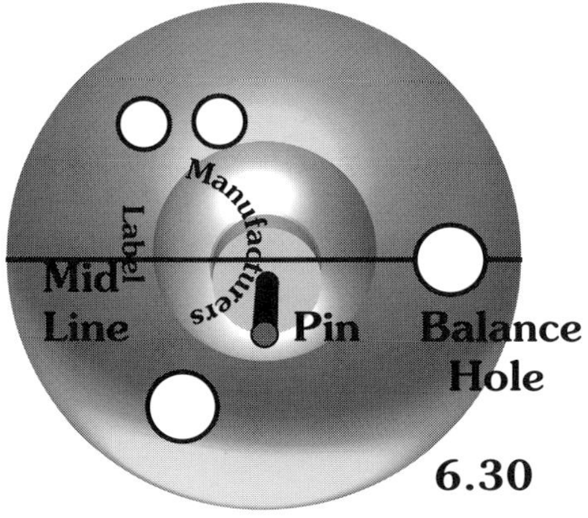


**Leverage Balance**
**Pin on the Mid Line**

## LEVERAGE BALANCE - EARLIER ROLL

1.) A Pin - Out ball is used and the pin is positioned below the leverage point (figure 6.30). This will provide an earlier roll with a moderate backend reaction.

2.) A Pin - In ball is used with the CG positioned on or below the mid line, and the pin being positioned below the leverage point. Once again, the balance hole can be drilled either on the axis point, or below the axis point based on the desired reaction and static balance. This drilling will provide an earlier roll with a backend reaction determined by the placement of the balance hole.

**** When using these pin down drillings, the ball track will be higher than normal due to the pin position. Therefore, these drillings are not usually recommended for players who track close to the thumb hole, as the ball track may roll over the thumb hole.***

**** Additionally, as these drillings initiate an earlier ball roll, less of the balls "energy" will be saved for the backends. Therefore, the backend reaction will be reduced when compared to the other examples using Leverage Balance.***

## LEVERAGE BALANCE - EVEN ROLL

1.) A Pin - Out ball is used and the pin is positioned on the leverage point. This will initially provide an initial even roll with a moderate to strong backend reaction.

2.) A Pin - In Ball is used with the pin and the CG being positioned on the leverage point (figure 6.31). The balance hole is positioned on the axis point or below the axis based on the desired reaction and static balance. This reaction will provide an initial even roll with the possibility of a stronger backend reaction than the "Pin - Out" example based on the position of the balance hole.

**6.32 - Leverage Balance Reaction - Right-Handed Version**

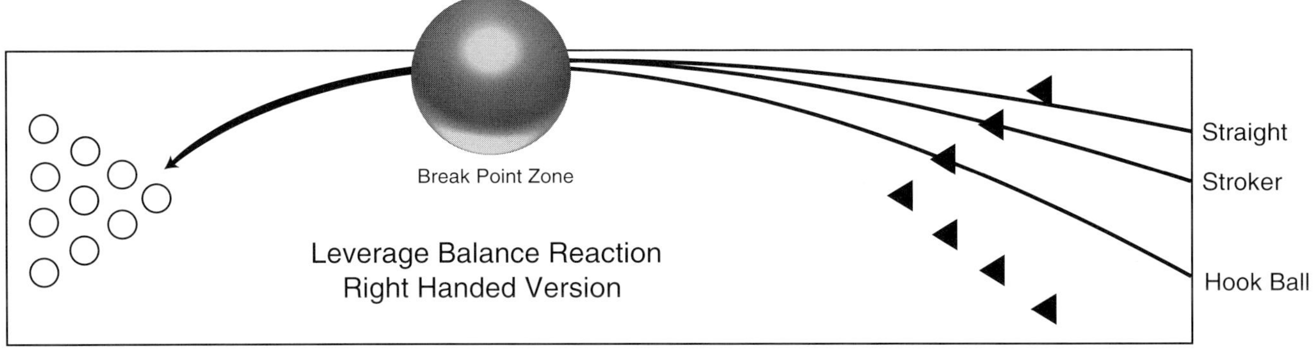


**6.32 - Leverage Balance Reaction - Left-Handed Version**

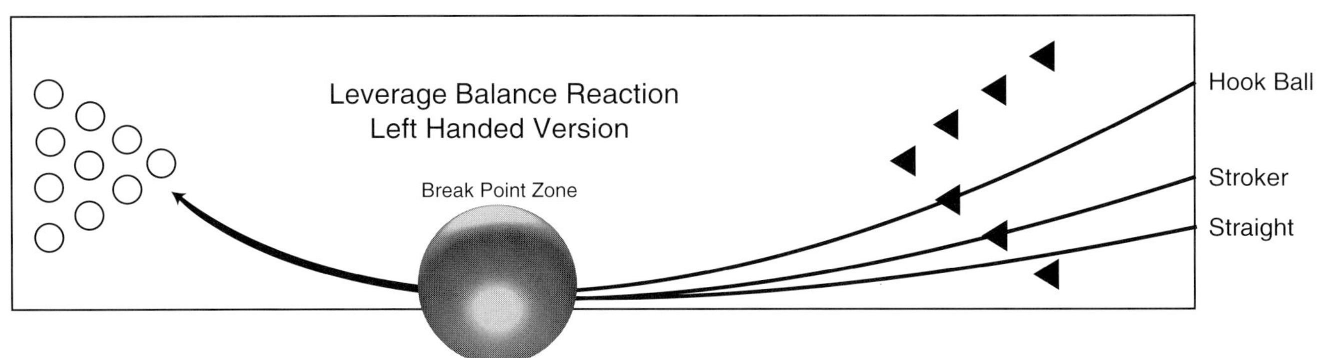


# AXIS BALANCE

Axis Balance, when compared to Label and Leverage Balance, is the least common of the three. The reason being that most bowlers will only use this balance on a select few lane conditions. However, when this balance is needed it can be very effective.

The name Axis Balance is derived from the position of the weight block in this balance. Here, the pin is placed on the axis point, positioning the entire weight block around the axis line (figure 6.33). Therefore, recalling weight block stability example #2, the ball will initiate an earlier roll then either Label or Leverage Balance.

**Axis Balance**

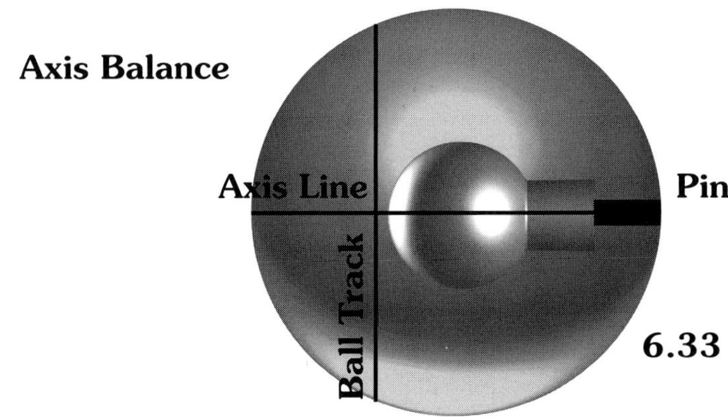

The detriment to Axis Balance deals with the use of the balls energy. As explained earlier, a ball which is balanced to roll early can sometimes use its energy completely before it reaches the pins. When this occurs the ball is said to be "rolled out."

To avoid the ball rolling out, Axis Balance must be used on the appropriate conditions, and combined with the proper surface. There are two conditions in which Axis Balance is very beneficial. These are;

Heavy Oil Conditions
or
Very "Spotty" Conditions

The reason for this balance on both of these conditions is that Axis Balance rolls even, and provides moderate to minimal backend reaction. Therefore, on a very oily condition, a washed cover with Axis Balance is advantageous as the ball will have the greatest chance to pick up an early roll, and will not overreact on the backends.

In the same fashion, a shiny cover matched with Axis Balance will work well on conditions in which the oil appears scattered and unbalanced on the lane. In this example, the polished surface will help the ball to initially skid, and the Axis Balance once again will provide an even backend reaction. When combined, these factors create a very controllable ball for usually difficult lane conditions.

## BALANCE HOLES

When drilling Axis Balance, there will most always be the need for a balance hole to make the ball statically legal. Once again, where the balance hole is drilled will have a direct effect on how the ball will react.

As a general rule, the balance hole will be positioned below the axis point. The reason being that if the hole is drilled on the axis point, therefore through the pin, the hole will remove the majority of the top of the weight block. Axis Balance (depending on the weight blocks design) usually depends on the top of the weight block to provide a percent of its backend reaction. Therefore, by removing this portion of the block, the ball will have an even roll with very little backend reaction.

Thus it is usually most beneficial to drill the balance hole below the axis point. Once again, the exact position of the balance hole will be determined based on the desired ball reaction, and the desired static balance.

## BALL REACTION USING AXIS BALANCE

As a general rule, Axis Balance is drilled with the pin positioned on the axis point, with the Center of Gravity located on the axis line. This is accomplished with either a "Pin - In" or "Pin - Out" ball. The reaction characteristics of both are very similar.

## *AXIS BALANCE - "PIN - IN"*

Once again the pin is positioned on the axis point, with the CG positioned on the mid line (figure 6.34). The balance hole is drilled only slightly below the axis point for even and early roll, while slightly more skid and backend reaction can be achieved by drilling the balance hole 9 inches from the center of the grip (or 3 3/8ths of an inch below the axis point).

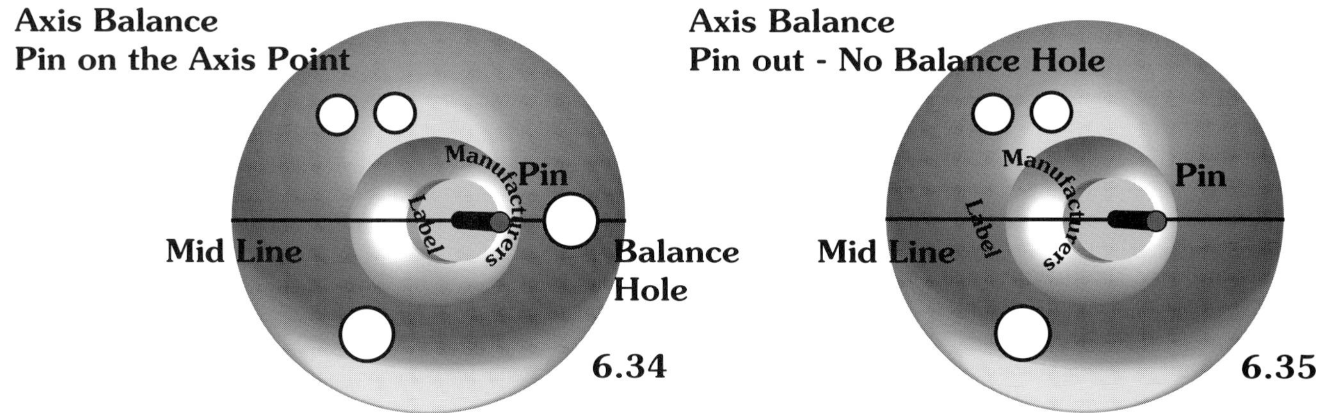


## *AXIS BALANCE - "PIN - OUT"*

In figure 6.35, the pin is placed on the axis point with the CG being positioned on the mid line closer to the label area. When drilled in this position, the ball will have a more even reaction as it rolls down the lane, with slightly less backend reaction. This is the result of positioning the weight block in a stable balance, without the use of a balance hole.

**6.36 - Right-Handed Version**

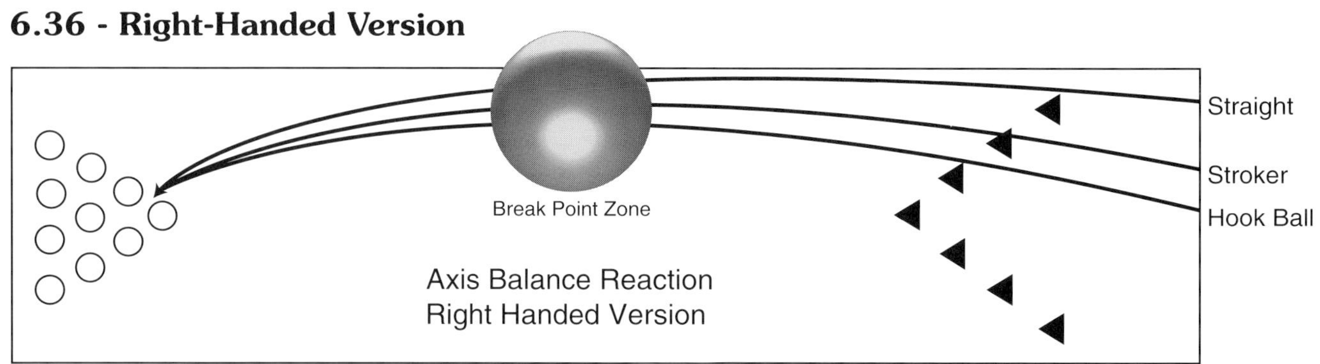


**6.36 - Left-Handed Version**

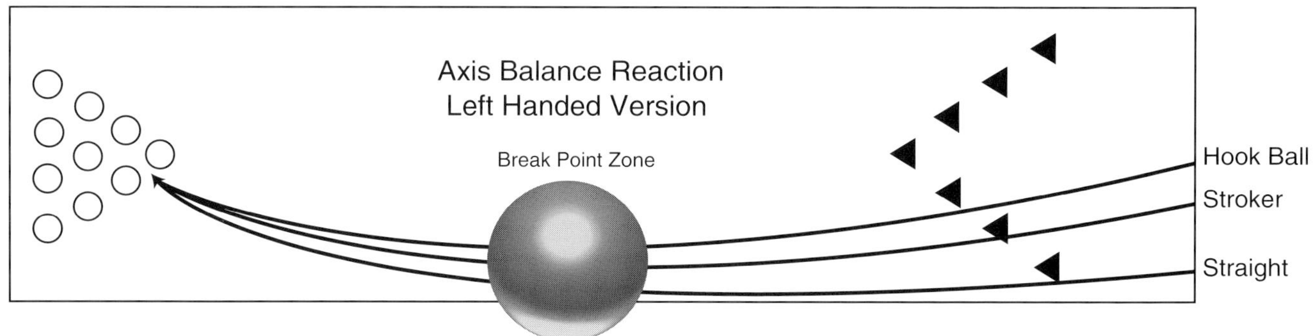

In both of these examples, the overall reaction will be an initial early roll with moderate to minimal backend reaction. However, the Pin - Out drilling, with the balance hole drilled in the 9 inch position, should provide the strongest backend reaction of these two examples.

## LEVERAGE AXIS BALANCE

As you can imagine, there are more ways to balance a bowling ball than just Label, Leverage and Axis Balance. One of the more popular methods, with reactive resin bowling balls, is to position the weight block between the leverage and axis points (figure 6.37).

By positioning the block in this fashion, the ball will have reaction characteristics of each balance. It will generally have an in initial early and even roll, similar to Axis Balance, combined with a moderate backend reaction (usually considered to react stronger than Axis Balance, but not as strong as Leverage Balance).

This has become a very useful balance on lanes with a longer oil pattern with strong backends. The Leverage - Axis Balance helps to tame this usually "over -under" reacting condition. This is accomplished by the ball initially rolling early to combat the oil, yet providing moderate and even backend reaction to control the dry backends.

The reason for the moderate backend reaction is due to the Stability of the weight block. In the case of Leverage weight, the block is at a 45 degree angle from the axis line. This makes the block unstable, and promotes a strong backend reaction.

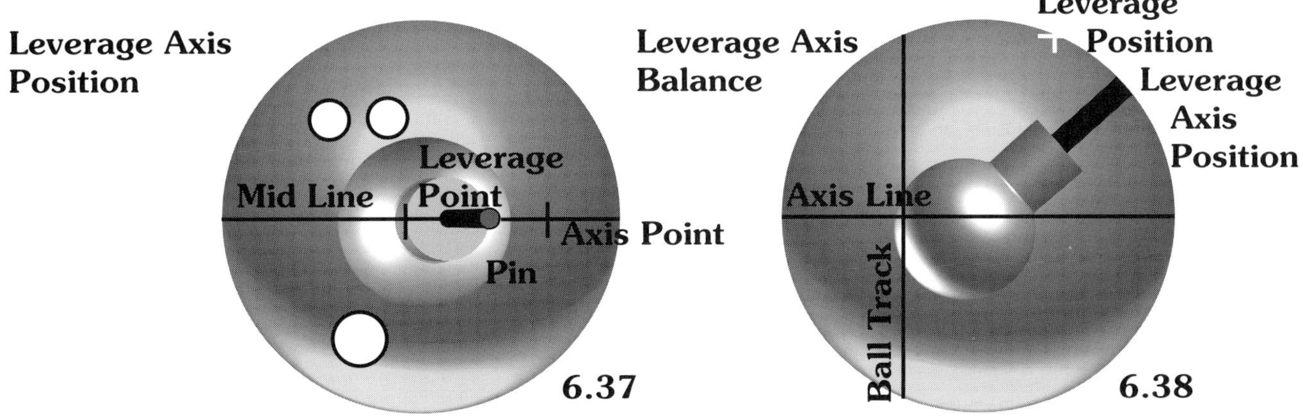


However, Leverage - Axis is usually positioned between the leverage and axis points, creating an angle of approximately 20 - 25 degrees. (figure 6.38) In this position the weight block is still unstable, however, it is still in a more stable or balanced position than Leverage Balance. Thus the backend reaction is less.

As always, the position of the balance hole will influence the bowling balls overall reaction as it rolls down the lane.

# BALL REACTION USING LEVERAGE AXIS BALANCE

Leverage Axis Balance can be drilled with the pin above, below, or on the mid line for desired reactions. Usually the CG will be positioned on the mid line in either the Pin - In or Pin Out drilling.

## *LEVERAGE AXIS - LONGER SKID*

The CG is positioned on the mid line, and the pin is situated above the leverage axis point (figure 6.39). This will provide a reaction of initial skid combined with moderate backend reaction.

## *LEVERAGE AXIS - EARLY ROLL*

The CG is placed on the mid line, with the pin being placed below the leverage axis point (figure 6.40). This provides a reaction of initial early roll combined with minimal to moderate backend reaction.

**It is important to remember that having the pin placed below the mid line will cause the ball use its energy early, and will therefore reduce the backend reaction.*

**Also, this early roll will raise the ball track, and therefore should be used cautiously with high track players.*

**Leverage Axis Balance**
**Pin Above the Mid Line**

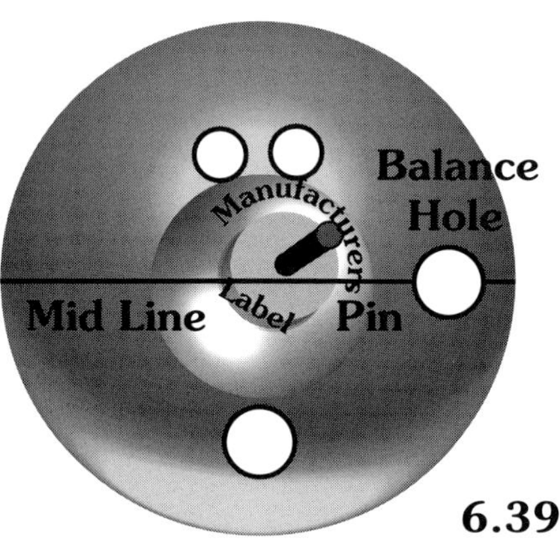

**6.39**

**Leverage Axis Balance**
**Pin Below the Mid Line**

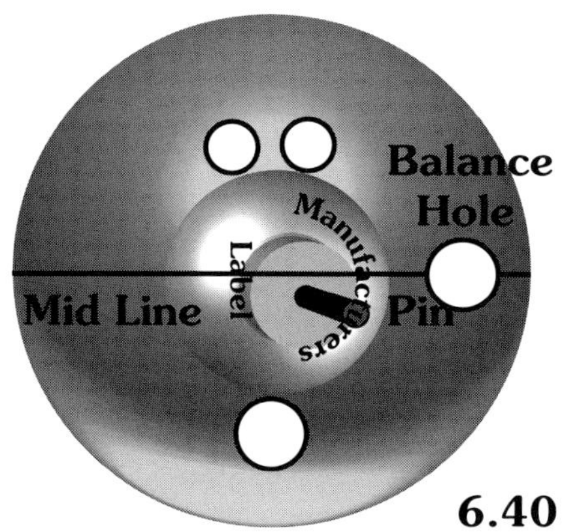

**6.40**

**Leverage Axis Balance**
**Pin on The Mid Line**

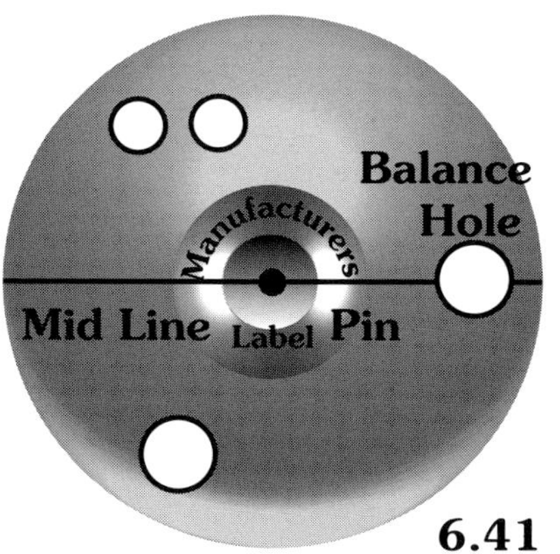

**6.41**

## LEVERAGE AXIS - EVEN ROLL

In this example, both the pin and the CG are positioned on the mid line, with the pin being placed on the Leverage Axis point (figure 6.41). This will provide an initial even roll, with moderate backend reaction.

***In each of these examples, it is important to remember that the exact position of the CG and the balance hole will have an influence on the overall reaction of the ball as it rolls down the lane.***


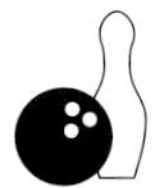

### 6.42 - Leverage Axis Balance Reaction - Right-Handed Version

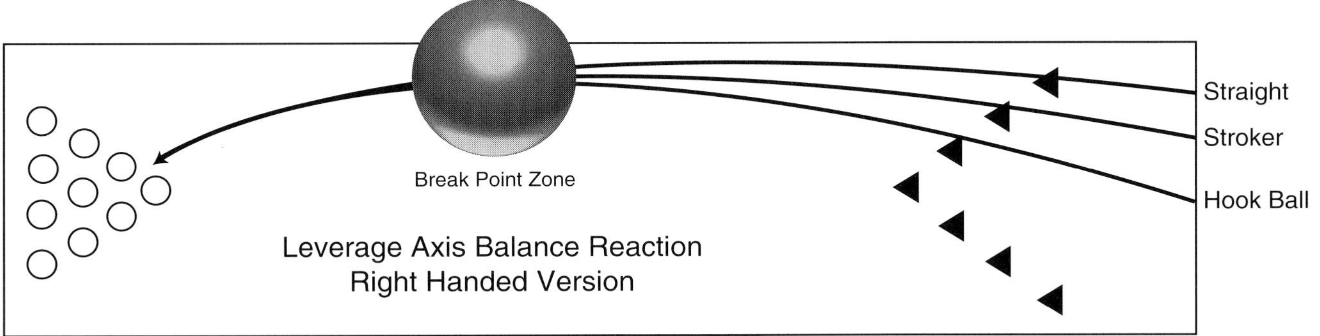


### 6.42 - Leverage Axis Balance Reaction - Left-Handed Version

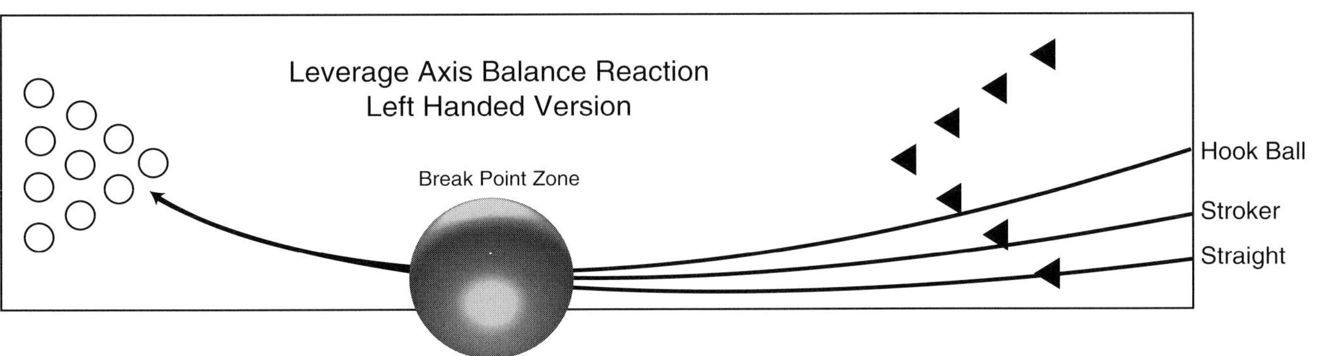


## MATCHING DYNAMIC BALANCE TO LANE CONDITIONS

This chapter has covered an abundance of material, and has shown a variety of methods for drilling bowling balls. Therefore, lets look at how each type of player (Hook Ball, Stroker or Straight Player) will use these balances for specific lane conditions.

For the purpose of identifying lane conditions, the following distances will be assumed.

* Dry Lanes are considered to be oiled 18 - 25 feet or less
* Medium Lanes are considered to be oiled 25 - 35 feet
* Oily Lanes are considered to be oiled 35 - 45 feet or more

## STRAIGHT PLAYER

In review, the Straight Player will have average to above average ball speed with minimal backend hook (5 Boards or less). Therefore, the following balances would be recommended for the Straight Player on these conditions;

***Dry Lanes*** = *Label Balance or Leverage Balance*

As the lane condition is providing a good amount of hook, the Straight Player will be able to use a ball with a strong balance. Label Balance with the pin on or above the mid line, and "out" would usually be a good combination. Also Leverage Balance would be suitable, provided the lane has oil in the heads, creating initial skid.

***Medium Lanes*** = *Label Balance, Axis Balance or Leverage Axis Balance*

In this example the lanes have a longer oil condition, and the Straight Player needs to initiate an earlier roll. Therefore, Label Balance, with the pin below the mid line would help to achieve this roll. Also, and most likely, the most beneficial would be Axis Balance. Here the ball will certainly initiate the earlier roll, with minimal backend reaction. For slightly more backend reaction than Axis Balance, this player could also use Leverage Axis Balance.

***Oily Lanes*** = *Axis Balance*

As it is imperative for the Straight Player to achieve an early roll on this condition, Axis Balance would be the solution. This will give the player the best chance for a slight break on the backends, and should create a heavy rolling action as the ball contacts the pins.

## STROKER PLAYER

As previously mentioned, the Stroker Player is considered to have medium ball speed with a backend reaction of 5 - 10 boards of hook. Given these factors, the following balances would be recommended for the Stroker Player on these conditions;

***Dry Lanes*** = *Label or Axis Balance*

Given a shorter oil condition, a ball which is stable would most likely be the best choice. Label Balance with the pin only slightly "out" and positioned above the mid line would be a good choice. Also, if the condition is "spotty" or unbalanced, a highly polished Axis Balance ball would not be a bad choice, as this will react very evenly, and should be controllable on this difficult condition.

***Medium Lanes*** = *Label, Leverage or Leverage Axis Balance*

Medium lanes usually represent a very high scoring condition. Therefore, to create "Area" on this condition, either a "Pin - Out" Label Balanced ball or Leverage Balance (usually keeping the CG on the mid line in both cases) will be the best choices to exploit this condition. In addition, if the lanes are medium but over reactive (excessively dry backends) Leverage Axis would be the balance of choice. This will "tame" the backend reaction, but still provide sufficient hook.

**Oily Lanes** = *Label, Axis or Axis Leverage Balance*

On this condition, the Stroker needs the ball to initiate an early roll to provide for sufficient backend reaction. Therefore, Label Balance with the pin below the mid line and slightly out would be a good choice. Also, Axis Balance will provide an earlier roll, with slightly less backend reaction which can be beneficial on this condition. Leverage Axis could also be used provided the ball will initiate an early roll on the condition.

## HOOK BALL PLAYER

The Hook Ball Player is a bowler with average or above average ball speed, combined with a strong release which produces a backend hook of 10 boards or more. Based on this, the following balances would be recommended for this player on these conditions.

**Dry Lanes** = *Label Balance*

On this condition, the Hook Ball Player certainly needs a ball with a stable balance. The players release, combined with the dry lane condition will provide a strong reaction. Therefore, a Label Balanced ball with the pin in and above the mid line would be recommended. Also, the pin could be positioned close to the ball track for maximum skid if the lanes are excessively dry.

**Medium Lanes** = *Label, Leverage or Leverage Axis Balance*

Just as with the Stroker Player, the Hook Ball Player should be able to create a fair amount of area on this condition. Therefore, Label Balance with the pin out or Leverage Balance (with the pin above the mid line in both cases) should provide initial skid with strong backend reaction. If the condition is over reactive, Leverage Axis could be used to maintain an even roll providing a more consistent backend reaction.

**Oily Lanes** = *Label, Leverage, Axis or Leverage Axis Balance*

Depending on the exact condition, any of the balances could be used. Label Balance with the pin slightly out and below the mid line (CG on the mid line) would be a good choice. In addition, Axis or Leverage Axis Balance could be used for an earlier roll with less backend reaction. Also, if the bowler chooses to create area, a dull surfaced Leverage Balanced ball (with the pin and CG on the mid line) could be used. The key is for the bowler to choose the balance which best suites his game, and matches the exact condition.

## CONCLUSIONS

Suffice it to say that there are many possible combinations which can be created to achieve a vast array of ball reactions. This is especially true when these dynamic balances are combined with Coverstocks, Surfaces, various Ball Constructions, and Static Balances.

**Dynamic Balance Combinations:**

| | Straight Player | Stroker | Hook Ball Player |
|---|---|---|---|
| **Dry Lanes** | Label Balance or Leverage Balance | Label Balance or Axis Balance | Label Balance |
| **Medium Lanes** | Label Balance or Axis Balance or Leverage Axis Balance | Label Balance or Leverage Balance or Leverage Axis Balance | Label Balance or Leverage Balance or Leverage Axis Balance |
| **Oily Lanes** | Axis Balance | Label Balance or Axis Balance or Leverage Axis Balance | Label Balance or Leverage Balance or Axis Balance or Leverage Axis Balance |

What is important for you is to determine what combination of these is best for you. That is what we will cover in our final chapter. How to put all of this information together, to produce a winning package for you!

# Chapter 7

The information throughout this book has been shown individually in relation to the Hook Ball, Stroker and Straight ball bowlers. In this chapter, all of the previous knowledge will be combined to produce a specific package for each of these players.

As mentioned in an earlier chapter, many bowlers carry 2 - 4 or more bowling balls, without knowing how they should react or on what conditions they should be used. This chapter will help to "put all the pieces together," and give you an edge when choosing the right bowling ball for a specific condition. This advantage certainly becomes invaluable in a tournament situation. Lets consider the following example;

*Bowler A is competing in a tournament with a limited number of games for qualifying - 3 games, and it is only a one day tournament. Therefore, it is very important to determine the correct equipment for the lane conditions as soon as possible. Fortunately, this player understands the reaction characteristics of each of his 4 bowling balls and determines which will be the best for the condition during his practice games.*

*On the contrary Bowler B brings his 4 bowling balls to the tournament, however does not have the same knowledge as Bowler A, and merely starts with his favorite bowling ball as usual. Over the course of his 3 games, Bowler B uses all 4 of his bowling balls searching for a suitable reaction, and does not match the right ball to the lane condition until the third game. In this situation Bowler A certainly has the advantage.*

The process which will be shown in this chapter will eliminate guess work, and help you to determine the correct ball for a given lane condition. In addition, an equipment "Game Plan" will be explained regarding how to rank your bowling balls. This becomes very useful in the event of having to change a ball during competition, and again eliminating the guesswork.

## MATCHING THE BALL TO THE LANE CONDITION

Each aspect of the bowling ball relates to a specific portion of the lane. This was briefly explained in Chapter 5 when static weights were shown to influence ball reaction in the Heads, Pine and Backends. In the same fashion all of the elements covered in this book will relate to a specific portion of the lane.

As a quick review, lets once again explain the three portions of the lane which we will study. These include;

*Heads* - The first 20 feet of the lane, starting at the foul line and extending to the area in which the pine begins.

*Pine* - The middle section of lane spanning 20 feet from the beginning of the pine (where the heads area ends) to approximately the 40 foot mark. Once again, the actual pine extends to the pin deck, but for our purposes we will consider the term "pine" to represent the middle 20 feet of the lane.

*Backends* - As the heads and pine represent the first 40 feet of the lane, the backends will represent the final 1/3 of the lane, or the last 20 feet.

The three elements of the bowling ball which will be compared to these sections of the lane are;

Surface Considerations
Ball Construction
Balance/Pin Position

The other two factors, coverstock and static weights also have an influence and will be included in our formula.

## HOW THEY MATCH UP

The following shows how each of these factors match.

Heads = Surface Characteristics

Pine = Ball Construction

Backends = Balance

Although each of these will have some overlapping benefits to different portions of the lane, this best represents the correlation of the bowling ball to the lane.

**7.1**

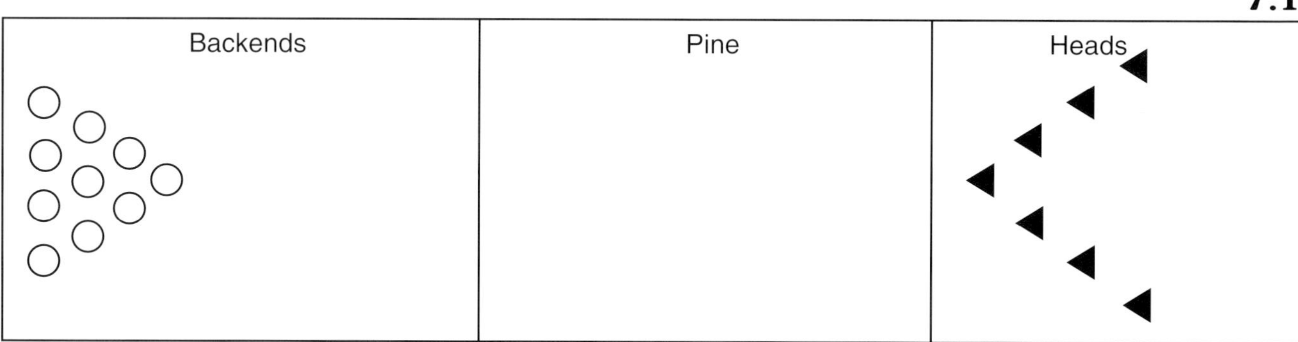

## HEADS - SURFACE CHARACTERISTICS

No matter how a bowling ball is constructed, or which balance is drilled into a ball, the surface will always have the greatest effect on the reaction of the ball through the heads. True, other elements will compliment the reaction, however surface will always have the greatest influence.

Therefore, an understanding of the three surfaces; Washed, Medium and Polished, becomes very useful when determining the correct ball surface for a given lane condition.

## PINE - BALL CONSTRUCTION

After the ball has passed through the heads area, where the surface was predominant, the ball now enters the pine, where ball construction provides the major influence.

As a general rule, the oil in the pine will usually not be as heavy as the oil in the heads (at least for a portion of the pine area). Therefore, as the oil usually decreases, the ball will react based on is inner construction.

Therefore, a ball with its mass close to the balls surface, such as a three piece design, will provide skid through this area of the lane. Conversely, a ball with its mass positioned towards the center of the ball, such as a two piece center heavy, design will provide a reaction of earlier roll through this portion of the lane.

## BACKENDS - BALL BALANCE

Although this would be an example of many factors contributing to ball reaction, balance has the greatest influence over ball reaction in this last 20 feet of the lane. Label, Leverage, Axis or Leverage Axis Balance will greatly determine the extent of the backend reaction.

Combined with these balances will be the position of the pin in relation to the balance. For example, if Label Balance is used, is the pin positioned above below or on the axis line? In addition is the pin "in" or "out." All of this together will more precisely determine the backend reaction.

Another element which is prevalent with today's bowling balls, is the effect of a polished reactive resin ball on the backend of the lane. Reactive resin provides a "tacky" feeling to the touch. This tackiness will translate into traction on the backend of the lane.

## REACTIVE RESIN VS URETHANE

Lets look at the following example comparing reactive resin to standard urethane, in regards to backend reaction.

Provided that the lane has sufficient oil in the first 30 feet to produce skid, the resin ball will be able to conserve its energy through this portion of the lane. However, as the ball rolls through the last 30 feet, the tacky cover will provide additional traction and contribute to the overall backend reaction when combined with the ball construction and balance.

Conversely, a polished urethane coverstock rolled on the same lane condition will produce different results on the back end of the lane. Here, when the urethane ball is polished, the ball will produce additional skid through the last half of the lane.

The reason these balls react differently is due to the coverstocks. A urethane coverstock, when polished, will have its traction reduced by the wax filling in the ridges, which decreases its hook. In effect, the balls surface becomes more smooth and therefore produces less overall traction.

In the same manner, the reactive resin cover also has its ridges filled with wax during the polishing process. The difference is the material of the coverstock. The resin ball will still retain the "Tacky" feeling after the polishing process, thus still providing traction on the backends.

## THE EQUIPMENT EQUATION

Now that we have matched the elements of a bowling ball to the appropriate portion of the lane, lets discover how we can produce bowling balls for specific conditions.

Without a doubt, the best way to analyze a lane is to break it down into the three previously mentioned sections, Heads, Pine, and Backends. This will be the basis for determining the best choice for a bowling ball on a given lane condition.

### EVALUATING THE HEADS

The first step in this process is to identify the conditions in the heads. The best way to accomplish this is to determine the balls reaction as it rolls through this part of the lane. Is the ball hooking or skidding through this area of the lane? Does the ball have a reaction of neither hook or skid, but even roll?

Once you have determined the reaction, you can associate the proper surface.

* *Remember, the medium surfaced ball is the best for testing lane conditions. This surface, combined with a two piece center heavy design with Label Balance will provide the best possible test ball and will be assumed in the following examples.*

***Lane #1***

You determine that the ball is rolling or hooking too much in the heads portion of the lane. Assuming the medium surfaced ball was used to test the lane, you can determine the need to change to a more polished surface. The extent of the surface change will be determined by how much the ball is hooking. In certain cases a change in coverstock will also be needed (for example, reactive resin to urethane).

 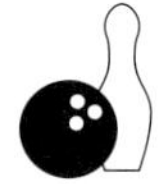

### *Lane #2*

In another example, the ball is skidding too much in the heads area. Here the change will be to a duller surface which will help the ball to gain an earlier roll. In the case of very heavy oil, a washed cover would be recommended.

### *Lane #3*

Finally, it is quite possible that the balls reaction in the heads is fine, but the problem appears to be in the pine or backends area. In this case, the medium surface would be used with a change to either the ball construction or balance.

## DETERMINING BALL REACTION IN THE PINE

Once the balls reaction has been determined in the heads, and the appropriate surface chosen, the next step is to complete a similar evaluation of the pines. Once again, factors such as early hook or extended skid will help in determining the needed reaction in this portion of the lane.

### *Lane #1*

In this example, it becomes obvious that the test ball is rolling too early, and not reaching the break point on the backends. Since the test ball uses a two piece center heavy ball, the bowler should change to a ball with more of its inner mass situated closer to the balls surface.

Therefore, a change to either a two piece cover heavy ball or a three piece ball would be the correct adjustment. The extent of skid needed would be determined by the bowler, and the appropriate weight block design chosen.

### *Lane #2*

On this condition, the ball is skidding too far in the pine area and skidding past the breakpoint on the backends. Since the test ball uses the earliest rolling weight block design, the balance would need to be adjusted to combat this condition.

As the test ball is drilled in a Label Balance position, a different balance for earlier roll, such as Axis Balance, could be used to initiate an earlier roll through the pines area of the lane.

### *Lane #3*

Here, the ball appears to roll through the middle portion of the lane without hook or skid problems. However, once the ball reaches its breakpoint, it hooks sharply on the backends and is uncontrollable.

In this example, the correction will once again be made in the balance of the ball. In this scenario, a ball which has a more stable balance would be the choice.

## CREATING THE OPTIMAL BACKEND REACTION

After determining the ball reaction through the first two sections of the lane, the backends represents the final adjustment. At this point, the ball has reached its breakpoint and the decision of ball reaction largely depends on how much hook is needed over the last 20 feet.

### *Lane #1*

The ball reaches its breakpoint but hooks very little on the last 20 feet of the lane. In this example, a balance which will create more backend reaction would be the choice.

Since the test ball is drilled with Label Balance, two possible solutions could be Leverage Balance or Leverage Axis Balance. In addition, provided a reactive ball can be used for the first 40 feet of the lane it would be recommended for increased backend reaction.

### *Lane #2*

Here, the ball reaches its breakpoint, but has inconsistent reaction on the backends. This would require a ball with a stable balance and a very even and predictable roll.

Either a Pin - In Label Balance or Axis Balance (the more probable solution) would be suggested. Axis Balance would provide a very even roll, and usually will not overreact. Also, changing the coverstock to urethane from reactive resin will help to regain control on an unstable lane condition.

### *Lane #3*

This final example finds the ball reaching its breakpoint but hooking very sharply on the backend. Once again, a stable balance would be required for less reaction.

Two possible solutions in this example would be Label Balance drilled with the Pin - In, or Leverage Axis Balance. Both of these would help to smooth the backend reaction, with Leverage Axis possibly being used in a urethane cover for greater control.

# MATCHING THE BOWLER, BALL AND LANE CONDITION

We now have a method to evaluate a lane condition. Thus, we can now apply this knowledge to practical conditions, based on the type of bowler we are. In this section, 4 different lane conditions will be covered along with the appropriate bowling ball for each type of player.

The recommendations in this section are provided as a guideline, not as the rule. Therefore, there will be various combinations for each player, to enable good ball reaction on each condition. Also, these recommendations will be kept in general terms. If you need clarification or more specific information in a certain area, please review the previous chapters to make the exact determination of your needs for a specific condition.

# LANE CONDITION #1

* A fresh oil condition with 40 feet of oil (oil to 35 feet and buffed to 40 feet), and dry backends

This condition represents a common condition which would be encountered at the beginning of a tournament. Given the condition, lets evaluate the 3 areas of the lane to determine the type of ball needed.

Heads = Oily
Pine = Medium Oily to Oily
Backends = Dry

The following information represents combinations of all the elements covered in this book, to provide the best bowling ball for each player on this condition.

## *STRAIGHT PLAYER*

Surface = Washed
Ball Construction = Two Piece Center Heavy
Balance = Axis
Static Weights = Bottom Weight, Thumb Weight, and Right Side Weight
Coverstock = Reactive Resin or Urethane

This combination will provide an early roll, with a small backend reaction, thus allowing the Straight Player to be competitive on this condition.

## *STROKER PLAYER*

Surface = Dull or Washed
Ball Construction = Two Piece Center Heavy
Balance = Label, Axis or Axis Leverage
Static Weights = Zero Balance or Bottom Weight, Thumb Weight, Right Side Weight
Coverstock = Reactive Resin or Urethane

This combination has a few variables, giving the player more options when selecting the bowling ball.

## *HOOK BALL PLAYER*

Surface = Medium to Dull
Ball Construction = Two Piece Center or Cover Heavy
Balance = Label, Leverage, Axis or Axis Leverage
Static Weights = Zero Balance or Top Weight, Zero Balance or Finger Weight, Zero Balance or Right Side Weight
Coverstock = Reactive Resin or Urethane

Once again, this combination provides the Hook Ball Player with many options. This is due to the area this player can create, because of his release. Therefore, the exact combination depends upon how the player chooses to play the lane condition.

## LANE CONDITION #2

A medium lane condition with 25 feet of oil buffed to 32 feet. The backends on this condition are dry.

This represents a very common league condition. It would be considered a medium condition, and also should produce a good scoring environment. Lets once again evaluate the three areas of the lane based on this condition.

Heads = Oily
Pine = Medium
Backends = Dry

### *STRAIGHT PLAYER*

Surface = Dull Washed
Ball Construction = Two Piece Center Heavy
Balance = Label, Axis or Axis Leverage
Static Weights = Bottom Weight or Zero Balance, Thumb Weight or Zero Balance, Right Side Weight
Cover Stock = Reactive Resin or Urethane

Here, the Straight Player can anticipate an early roll, with slightly increased hook on the backends. This combination should provide a favorable overall reaction on this condition.

### *STROKER PLAYER*

Surface = Medium to Polished
Ball Construction = Two Piece Center Heavy or Two Piece Cover Heavy
Balance = Label, Leverage or Leverage Axis
Static Weights = Top Weight or Zero Balance, Finger Weight, Zero Balance or Thumb Weight, Right Side Weight
Coverstock = Reactive Resin or Urethane

This condition will provide the Stroker Player an opportunity to create "area," thus leading to a chance for higher scores.

### *HOOK BALL PLAYER*

Surface = Polished
Ball Construction = Two Piece Center Heavy or Two Piece Cover Heavy
Balance = Label, Leverage or Leverage Axis
Static Weights = Top Weight, Finger Weight, Right Side Weight
Coverstock = Reactive Resin or Urethane

The Hook Ball Player will need longer skid on this condition, with controlled backend reaction. This combination should provide these elements, and once again create a larger target area to enable higher scores.

## LANE CONDITION #3

A dry lane condition with oil to 20 feet and buffed to 25 feet. Once again the backends are dry.

This represents the "Short Oil" condition of the mid to late 1980's. This condition could also represent a lane condition which might have started with oiling similar to the #2 condition. However, after many games have been played the oil will be absorbed into the lane (provided it is a wood surface), evaporated and be picked up on the ball. These factors will all create a dry lane condition.

Heads = Medium - Oily
Pine = Dry
Backends = Dry

### *STRAIGHT PLAYER*

Surface = Medium to Polished
Ball Construction = Two Piece Center Heavy or Two Piece Cover Heavy
Balance = Label or Leverage
Static Weights = Zero Balance or Top Weight, Zero Balance or Finger Weight, Right Side Weight
Coverstock = Reactive Resin or Urethane

The Straight Player will most likely see his biggest overall reaction on this condition. Given this combination, the ball will initially skid, but provide a strong backend reaction. This should provide a high scoring environment for this player on the dry lane conditions.

### *STROKER PLAYER*

Surface = Polished to Highly Polished
Ball Construction = Two Piece Cover Heavy or Three Piece
Balance = Label or Axis
Static Weights = Top Weight, Finger Weight, Zero Balance or Right Side Weight
Coverstock = Urethane or Reactive Resin

The Stroker Player will need to have a ball that will reach the break point, but not overreact on the backends. This combination should help to tame the lane reaction, but still provide high scores.

### *HOOK BALL PLAYER*

Surface = Highly Polished
Ball Construction = Two Piece Cover Heavy or Three Piece

Balance = Label Balance
Static Weights = Top Weight, Finger Weight, Right Side Weight, Zero Balance or Left Side Weight
Coverstock = Urethane or Polyester

Since this lane condition is providing 35 feet of backend hook, this Player must be concerned with skidding the ball far enough to reach his break point. The players release, combined with the dry backends, will still create backend reaction. Therefore, the above combination should help to control this condition, which can be accomplished without reactive resin!

## LANE CONDITION #4

This is a condition which is seen after the lane has been bowled on for a number of games. Here, the oil has been carried down the lane, and the heads are hooking. This is a common tournament condition later in the day. Initially, the condition might start with a pattern similar to the #1 or #2 example above. However, over the course of the day, the oil will break down and be carried down the lane.

It is important to consider these 2 factors on this condition;

1.) The ball must not hook early in the heads
2.) The ball must begin to roll through the pines, to ensure a backend reaction

Also, depending on the bowler, the backend reaction will usually be minimal. This is due to oil still being present on the backends. As this is the normal "Hook Area", the oil will greatly reduce the amount of backend reaction on this condition. Therefore, it is important to begin the ball rolling through the pine, for if the ball skids too long in the pine, it will never recover to hook on the backends.

Heads = Medium to Dry
Pine = Medium to Oily
Backends = Medium to Oily

### *STRAIGHT PLAYER*

Surface = Medium to Dull
Ball Construction = Two Piece Center Heavy
Balance = Axis
Static Weights = Zero Balance or Thumb Weight, Zero Balance or Right Side Weight
Coverstock = Reactive Resin or Urethane

This condition calls for the Straight Player to use a bowling ball which will begin a roll through the middle portion of the lane, and provide a small backend reaction. This combination should provide the needed reaction.

### *STROKER PLAYER*

Surface = Medium
Ball Construction = Two Piece Center Heavy
Balance = Label, Axis or Axis Leverage
Static Weights = Zero Balance or Top Weight, Thumb Weight or Zero Balance, Right Side Weight or Zero Balance
Coverstock = Reactive Resin or Urethane

Here, the Stroker needs to be concerned with rolling the ball through the heads without it hooking early, but still maintain an early roll through the pines. By creating the early roll through the pine, this bowler will have a good chance of backend reaction.

### *HOOK BALL PLAYER*

Surface = Medium to Slightly Polished
Ball Construction = Two Piece Center Heavy or Two Piece Cover Heavy
Balance = Label, Axis or Leverage Axis
Static Weights = Top Weight or Zero Balance, Thumb Weight or Zero Balance, Right Side Weight or Zero Balance
Coverstock = Reactive Resin or Urethane

The Hook Ball Player must be concerned with the same factors as the Stroker. This is especially true with skidding the ball through the heads, and still maintaining an early roll through the pine. Due to this players strong release, he will have the best chance to create backend reaction, provided the ball begins to roll early enough.

These examples are based on the concept that we can create a bowling ball for a given condition. This is a tremendous method of evaluating lane conditions, and determining the specific combination for your game on a certain condition. However, this scenario is not always possible in most situations.

Therefore, you must determine the ball in your package which best relates to the ball needed for the condition.

## WHAT IS THE RIGHT PACKAGE FOR YOU?

As we have mentioned throughout this book, many bowlers carry 2, 4, 6 or more bowling balls to leagues and tournaments. But how do you determine what bowling balls to carry in this set?

One prerequisite for this package is that all of the bowling balls should be different, to cover a broad range of conditions. In addition, you should be able to rank your bowling balls based on how they react. The best method is to rank them starting from the ball which hooks the most, to the ball which hooks the least.

## RANKING YOUR BOWLING BALLS

The "Ranking System" will allow you to change balls as the conditions warrant, and eliminate guesswork as to how each ball will react.

If you carry 4 bowling balls, the following order could be used;

### *BALL #1 - OILY CONDITION*

Surface = Washed
Ball Construction = Two Piece Center Heavy
Balance = Axis
CoverStock = Reactive Resin

### *BALL #2 - MEDIUM - OILY CONDITION*

Surface = Medium
Ball Construction = Two Piece Center Heavy
Balance = Leverage
Coverstock = Reactive Resin

### *BALL #3 - MEDIUM - DRY CONDITION*

Surface = Polished
Ball Construction = Two Piece Cover Heavy
Balance = Label
Coverstock = Reactive Resin

### *BALL #4 - DRY CONDITION*

Surface = Highly Polished
Ball Construction = Three Piece
Balance = Label
Static Weights = Top Weight, Finger Weight, Right Side Weight
Coverstock = Urethane

As all of these balls will react differently, it becomes easy to rank them and to know how to change equipment as the conditions warrant.

For example,

*You might start a tournament with ball #1, as the lanes are very oily. However, after a number of games, you find that the first ball is hooking too early, as the oil is beginning to be carried down and absorbed into the lane (wood surface). Therefore, you would change to Ball #2, to regain a favorable reaction.*

*As this is a tournament where you need to come back for another squad, you might find the lanes fairly dry, and need to start with Ball #3 (especially if the lanes are not oiled*

*between your squad times). As you bowl, the lanes become drier, and you determine the need for a ball which is more controllable. Thus, you change to Ball #4 for more consistent reaction and control on the dry lanes.*

In this example, it is shown that you will have to use all 4 bowling balls over the course of the tournament. Since all the balls have been designed for different conditions, and have been ranked based on their reaction characteristics, the choices become much easier.

Keep in mind that this is simply an example of a 4 ball package. Your set might very well be different. However, you need to rank them in a similar manner. Also, this should be updated on a continual basis, as new bowling balls are added to or subtracted from your package.

# DESIGN A WINNING PACKAGE

The following represents suggested packages for the Straight Player, Stroker and Hook Ball Players. These sets are based on a two ball package and a four ball package, and have been determined by the knowledge presented through this book.

## STRAIGHT PLAYER

**Ball #1**

Surface = Washed
Ball Construction = Two Piece Center Heavy
Balance = Axis
Coverstock = Reactive Resin

**Ball #2**

Surface = Medium
Ball Construction = Two Piece Center Heavy
Balance = Label
Coverstock = Reactive Resin

**Ball # 3**

Surface = Medium
Ball Construction = Two Piece Center Heavy
Balance = Leverage Axis
Coverstock = Reactive Resin

**Ball #4**

Surface = Polished
Ball Construction = Two Piece Center Heavy
Balance = Leverage
Coverstock = Reactive Resin

* If a two ball set is desired, Ball #1 and #3 would be chosen.

This package should provide the Straight Player diversity in ball reaction, as well as match his game on a variety of lane conditions.

## STROKER PLAYER

### *Ball #1*

Surface = Washed
Ball Construction = Two Piece Center Heavy
Balance = Axis
Coverstock = Reactive Resin

### *Ball #2*

Surface = Medium
Ball Construction = Two Piece Center Heavy
Balance = Label
Coverstock = Reactive Resin

### *Ball #3*

Surface = Polished
Ball Construction = Two Piece Center Heavy
Balance = Leverage
Coverstock = Reactive Resin

### *Ball #4*

Surface = Highly Polished
Ball Construction = Two Piece Cover Heavy
Balance = Label
Coverstock = Urethane

* Balls #2 and 3 would be suggested for a 2 ball set

This package should provide the Stroker with bowling balls to cover a wide variety of lane conditions, while matching his particular style.

## HOOK BALL PLAYER

### *Ball #1*

Surface = Dull
Ball Construction = Two Piece Center Heavy
Balance = Axis Leverage
Coverstock = Reactive Resin

***Ball #2***

Surface = Slightly Polished
Ball Construction = Two Piece Center Heavy
Balance = Leverage
Coverstock = Reactive Resin

***Ball #3***

Surface = Polished
Ball Construction = Two Piece Cover Heavy
Balance = Label
Coverstock = Reactive Resin

***Ball #4***

Surface = Highly Polished
Ball Construction = Three Piece
Balance = Label
Coverstock = Urethane

* If a two ball set is desired, balls #1 and 3 would be recommended.

Once again, this package provides diversity and would be best suited for the Hook Ball Player on a variety of lane conditions.

## CONCLUSION

Remember, these are only suggestions! Your specific package will depend on Lane Conditions on which you compete most frequently, and your particular style. However, this should provide a basis for determining your package.

Also, for those bowlers desiring to carry more than 4 bowling balls, you must consider the following factors;

1.) Evaluate your game and the lane conditions upon which you will be bowling.
2.) Add bowling balls to your package based on the existing balls, and those needed for other conditions.
3.) Always "rank" the new balls along with the existing ones to avoid confusion.

Once this has been completed, you will be ready for competition, and the equipment 1/5th of your game will be an asset to your overall bowling game.

# Final Conclusions

## Chapter 8

The information which has been presented in this book is to be taken in perspective. The bowling ball market has literally exploded with new equipment, and as a result, drilling techniques are quite frequently changing. Therefore, I encourage you to use these principles as a guideline for making your equipment decisions, not a rule.

As mentioned in the book, there are certainly more ways to drill bowling balls than I have covered. However, with the information provided, you have an infinite number of possible combinations by simply altering the following elements;

**Coverstocks**

Polyester
Urethane
Reactive Resin

**Surface**

Washed
Medium
Polished

**Ball Construction**

Three Piece
Two Piece Center Heavy
Two Piece Cover Heavy

**Balance**

Label
Leverage
Axis
Leverage Axis

**Pin**

"In" or "Out"
On, Above or Below the Mid Line

***This excludes the possible combinations which the addition of Static Weights and Balance Holes would produce.***

It is little wonder why bowlers often become confused with all of this information. However, I can only envision the market expanding further in the coming months and years. Innovative new coverstocks and weight block designs are being introduced at a rapid pace, and it is often difficult for the Pro Shops to keep up, not to mention the bowlers. Hopefully, the material we have covered will assist in understanding these new products.

# FIND A GOOD PRO SHOP

Now that you have advanced your knowledge of the equipment game, you need to find someone who is willing to work with you. In a perfect world, you could walk into any Pro Shop and ask for advice, or simply to have a ball drilled in a certain manner, without complication. However, this is not a perfect world and this does not always hold true.

I encourage you to seek out a Pro Shop that is willing to work with you through experimentation and in assembling your equipment package. If your current situation fits the bill, by all means stay with them. However, if you are having difficulties, change Pro Shops. There are plenty of quality businesses that would be willing to help.

When you find the right situation, please remember the following;

1) Respect the persons time.
2) Do not ask for unrealistic prices or discounts.
3) Don't make the Pro Shop your personal "hang out."
4) Take care of the staff.

If you want to maintain a good working atmosphere with your Pro Shop, these factors need to be taken seriously. You will gain their respect as a customer, and they will provide you with the service you desire.

## KEEP IT SIMPLE, AND HAVE FUN!

There are many levels of bowlers in our great sport. Regardless of your status, always remember that equipment is only 1/5th of the complete bowlers equation. A new bowling ball will never make up for needed games of practice or a deficiency in your physical bowling game.

Every good athlete evaluates their strengths and weaknesses when striving to improve. Bowlers are no different. If you have difficulties with any facet of your game, I highly recommend consulting a creditable instructor for the solution. They will be able to review your game and suggest improvements which will hopefully take you to the next level.

The bottom line is to have fun! Ours is a great sport, but sometimes we make it too complicated. When this happens, people often begin to lose interest and quit. Don't let that happen to you! Keep bowling simple, and enjoy it to the fullest.

I wish you all the best, for many years of success and happiness in bowling.

**Axis Balance** - Describes a specific balance where the mass of the weight block surrounds the axis line and the top of the weight block. The pin, is positioned on the axis point.

**Axis Line** - The immaginary line which runs through the center of the ball and connects the two stable points, around which the weight block rotates. This is based on the bowlers Ball Track.

**Axis Point** - This is found based on the bowlers track. Specifically, the axis point is the end of the immaginary line around which the ball rotates as it travels down the lane, and is equidistant from all points of the ball track.

**Backends** - The last 20 feet of the lane, where the least amount of lane conditioner is found, and where a bowling ball usually makes its biggest break towards the pins.

**Balance Hole** - An extra hole drilled in a specific position in the bowling ball. This hole is used to balance the ball statically and alter the overall reaction of the ball as it rolls down the lane.

**Ball Track** - The portion of the ball which comes in contact with the lane as it rolls down the lane.

**Break Point** - That portion of the lane where the bowling ball completes its transition from skid to traction, and provides the greatest amount of hook. This generally occurs in the backend of the lane (the last 20 feet).

**Center of Gravity** - That position in which the ball is evenly balanced statically from right side to left side and from the finger quadrant to the thumb quadrant. This is usually indicted by the position of the label or a punch mark.

**Conventional Grip** - A type of grip which involves the insertion of the fingers to the second joint (from the nail), and the full insertion of the thumb. This is accomplished with the majority of the palm against the surface of the ball.

**Coverstock** - The outer shell of the bowling ball which can be constructed with a variety of materials such as Polyester, Rubber, or Urethane.

**Dynamic Balance** - Positioning the weight block in either a stable or unstable manner, to achieve a specific reaction as the ball rolls down the lane.

**Filler Material** - The material placed in a three piece ball to adjust for desired gross weight.

**Fingertip Grip** - A type of grip in which the fingers are inserted into the ball to the first joint (from the nail). Additionally, the majority of the palm is positioned against the ball and the thumb fully inserted into the thumb hole.

**Full Roller Track** - This represents a ball track which runs through the grip due to a particular release motion. (Outdated)

**Hard Rubber** - A type of Coverstock which is comprised of hard rubber, and produces a hard finish on the surface of the ball.

**Heads** - The portion of the lane which extends from the foul line, past the arrows, and to the pine. Usually, this is assumed to be the first 20 feet of the lane.

**Hole Size** - The size of the hole drilled to accommodate a particular bowlers fingers or thumb. Also used to determine ball reaction when used as a balance hole.

**Hook Ball Player** - A bowler with average to above average ball speed, combined with a strong release, creating a backend hook of 10 boards or more.

**Label Balance** - Describes a specific balance in which the bowlers grip is positioned over the Label engraving. The position of the weight block is determined by the CG for a three piece ball and the pin for a two piece ball.

**Leverage Axis Balance** - A specific Balance in which the pin, for a two piece ball, or the CG for a three piece ball, is positioned between the Axis Point and the Leverage Point. The exact position depends on the desired ball reaction.

**Leverage Balance** - Describes a specific balance in which the pin, for a two piece ball, or the CG, for a three piece ball, is positioned 3 3/8ths inches in from the axis point (towards the grip). The exact position depends upon the desired ball reaction.

**Leverage Point** - The position on the ball which is located 3 3/8ths inches in from the axis point (towards the grip) and on the axis line.

**Pin** - A polyester or urethane stem which is positioned in the weight block to hold the core in place as the coverstock is poured into the ball mold during the manufacturing process. Hence, this represents the top of the weight block.

**Pines** - The section of the lane which begins at approximately the 20 foot mark and expends to the pin deck. During lane play explanations, this represents the middle 20 feet of the lane.

**Pitches** - Angles in which grip holes are drilled, with the intent of matching a bowlers flexibility, and desired release action.

**Polyester** - A specific type of coverstock which is comprised of a plastic material with limited durability.

**Reactive Resin** - A coverstock comprised of similar materials used in the urethane formulation, however blended with different additives. This coverstock provides a "tacky" feeling which translates into additional traction, and usually strong backend reaction, as the ball advances towards the pins.

**Revolutions** - The number of times in which the weight block makes 1 full rotation around the axis line, as it rolls from the foul line to the head pin.

**Semi Fingertip Grip** - A type of grip in which the fingers are inserted to a position between the first and second joints (from the nail), with the thumb fully inserted. Due to the position of the fingers, the palm is not fully against the surface of the ball.

**Semi Roller Track** - Also known as the 3/4 roller, this ball track runs outside the grip in an area which is close to the fingers and thumb, to 2 - 3 inches from the grip.

**Soft Rubber** - A coverstock which is comprised of rubber and provides a softer cover for more traction as the ball rolls down the lane.

**Span** - The distance measured between the fingers and thumb.

**Spinner Track** - A ball track which runs 3 inches or below from the grip.

**Static Balance** - A method of balancing a bowling ball, on a static beam balance (scale), to determine the balance of weight when comparing equal halves of a bowling ball. Most effective with three piece weight blocks.

**Straight Player** - A bowler with average to above average ball speed, combined with minimal release action, creating a backend hook of 5 boards or less.

**Stroker Player** - A bowler with average to below average ball speed, combined with moderate release action, creating a backend hook of 5 - 10 boards.

**Three Piece Bowling Ball** - A bowling ball design comprised of three key elements; Coverstock, Filler Material, and a "Pancake Shaped" weight block. The common bowling ball design until the early 1980's.


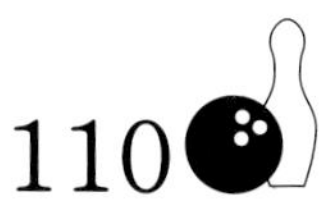

**Track Flare** - A wide ball track with many individual small tracks. This is created by an initial unstable weight block balance, which progresses to a stable position as the ball rolls down the lane.

**Two Piece Center Heavy Bowling Ball** - A bowling ball in which the weight block design concentrates its mass and density towards the center of the bowling ball. In addition to the weight block design, a coverstock is used, and thus comprises the two pieces. Other definitions include; Low Moment of Inertia, Low Mass, Core Heavy.

**Two Piece Cover Heavy Bowling Ball** - A bowling Ball in which the weight block is designed with its mass spread in a large area of the ball. This includes mass being positioned in the center of the ball, and also close to the balls surface. In addition to the weight block design, a coverstock is used, and thus comprises the two pieces. Other definitions include; High Moment of Inertia, High Mass, Shell Heavy.

**Urethane** - A coverstock comprised of material from the polymer family, which creates a hard and durable surface on the bowling ball.

**Weight Block** - The inner portion of the bowling ball which influences ball reaction based on its density and position.

**Weight Block Density** - The actual weight of the specific core configuration.

**World Class Bowler** - A highly versatile player with proven ability to win. The player has achieved this as a result of; a strong physical game, knowledge of lane play, a complete understanding of his "equipment package", an unprecedented mental game, and good physical maintenance.

# THE AUTHOR

Chip Zielke has been involved in the sport of bowling for the past 15 years. His career began 11 years ago as an on lanes instructor with the Professional Bowling Camps, and has led to International recognition as a World Class coach and instructor.

Chip has been involved in both the competitive side of the sport as an 8 year PBA member, and in the bowling industry as a consultant as well as an employee for two major bowling manufacturers. Also, he is a graduate of the College of St. Francis, with a B.S. in Marketing.

Recently, Chip held the position of National Bowling Coach for the Middle East country of Bahrain. During his tenure, the Bahrain Youth National Team captured the Gold medal in the GCC Youth Championships. The Bahrain Mens National Team was also very competitive in Regional and International competitions.

Throughout his career, Chip Zielke has been on the cutting edge of bowling technology. Through studying the technical aspects of the game with such masters as Ray Edwards, Fred Bordon and Don Johnson, he has developed a keen perspective for the sport. This has led to positions such as the Head Pro Shop Operator with the Professional Bowling Camps.

Today, Chip Zielke is a Pro Tour Consultant for a major bowling manufacturer. He also conducts leading edge seminars on coaching and bowling equipment both Nationally and Internationally.